TERRY DENTON'S
Really Truly Amazing
GUIDE TO
EVERY

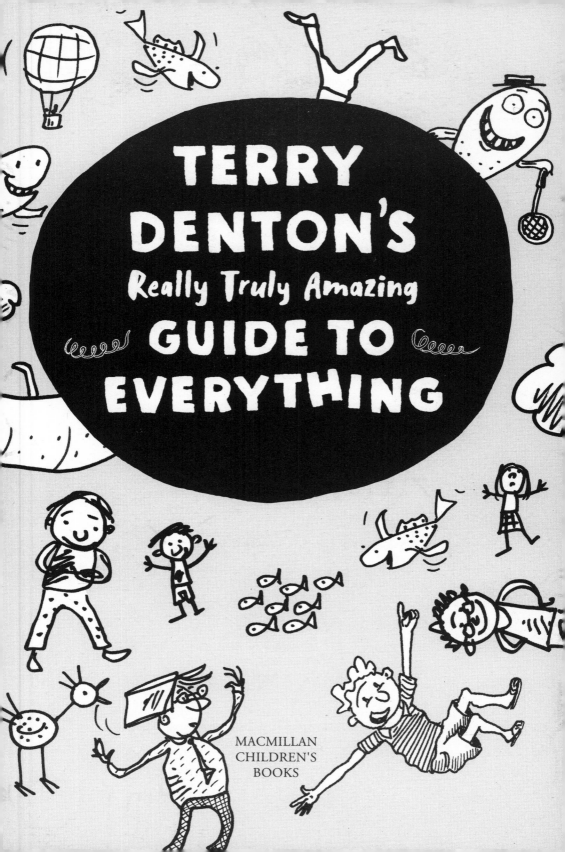

TERRY DENTON'S
Really Truly Amazing
GUIDE TO EVERYTHING

MACMILLAN
CHILDREN'S
BOOKS

First published by Puffin Books/Pengin Random House Australia 2014, 2020

This edition published in the UK 2021 by Macmillan Children's Books
an imprint of Pan Macmillan
The Smithson, 6 Briset Street, London EC1M 5NR
EU representative: Macmillan Publishers Ireland Limited,
Mallard Lodge, Lansdowne Village, Dublin 4
Associated companies throughout the world
www.panmacmillan.com

ISBN 978-1-5290-6603-6

1 3 5 7 9 8 6 4 2

A CIP catalogue record for this book is available from the British Library.

Printed and bound by CPI Group (UK) Ltd, Croydon CR0 4YY
Design by Tony Palmer © Penguin Random House Australia Pty Ltd

MIX
Paper from
responsible sources
FSC® C116313

DEDICATION!

For
KRISTEN

With thanks to
Michelle for
all the additional
research.

And Tony for
the design.

WHAT'S IN THIS BOOK

(Prepare to be amazed!)

A very serious and terribly important note from Professor Terry Denton

Chapter 1	You Are the Universe	2
Chapter 2	Your Planet Earth	30
Chapter 3	The Life Before You	66
Chapter 3½	The Life Around You	98
Chapter 4	The Universe In You	144
Chapter 5	The World We Made	176
Chapter 6	Time Flies	218
Chapter 7	I hope you were paying attention because there will be a test	254

A VERY SERIOUS AND TERRIBLY IMPORTANT NOTE FROM PROFESSOR

Terry Denton

Hi there, readers,

Most of us know a LITTLE BIT about a LOT of things.
Or a LOT about NOT MANY things.
But I know QUITE A BIT about ALMOST everything!

I bet you didn't even know
I was a professor.

Well, neither did I.

But I am!
My bird, my horse
and my giant spider said so.

In fact, everyone knows me as
the PROFESSOR OF ALMOST
EVERYTHING.

I'll admit, there's SOME stuff I know nothing about.

Stuff like make-up and fashion, car repair,
flying a plane, open-heart surgery,
closed-heart surgery and gorilla training . . .

But I looked all the OTHER STUFF up.

And I think you'll agree
that it's all VERY interesting.

In this book you will learn about:

THE UNIVERSE, which is very, very, very, very, very, very big.
It has billions of huge round things moving in (sort of) circles
around billions of other even huger round things.

PLANET EARTH, which is also very big
and full of flaming molten iron.
Yet somehow it doesn't burn up.

LIFE on Earth,
including weird animals like birds and horses,
and bugs and teeny weeny bacteria,
most of which are trying to eat you.

The HUMAN BODY and how the parts work . . . or don't work.
Or epically fail.

All the COOL STUFF that humans invented
and made with their brainy brains and fingery hands.

There's even a whole chapter about TIME,
except it's complicated,
and I don't understand any of it.
And after I have explained it, neither will you.

So stop reading my very serious and terribly important note
and start reading the . . .

Really Truly Amazing

GUIDE TO
EVERYTHING

And you will become a Professor of (almost) Everything too.

YOU ARE THE UNIVERSE

The Universe is BIG.
VERY BIG.

If you stood at the 'centre' of the Universe
the outer 'edge' would be an amazing
434,000,000,000,000,000,000,000 km away.

What a lot of kilometres!
That's why we say the Universe is

If you had a space car that could travel at 1,000 km
every second (THAT'S VERY FAST!) it would still take you
20,000,000,000,000 (20 trillion) years
to arrive at the far 'edge' of the Universe.

Hey, Bird, is
that the edge of
the Universe?

Space
Car

No, Horse,
that's the edge
of the page.

That's a VERY LONG TIME.
Far longer than the Universe has
been in existence.
And . . .
just to confuse you, no one knows if the Universe even has an edge.
Most scientists think that the Universe just keeps wrapping itself
around itself and that it's getting bigger.
It might keep expanding forever.

Even the smartest people in the world don't know for sure.

What is the Universe made of?
The Universe is mostly made of

NOTHING.

In our small solar system
even the distances between the planets are huge.
In 1977, the Voyager 2 spacecraft began a journey passing
all the planets. It took 12 years to arrive at Neptune,
the farthest planet from the Sun.
It was travelling at 56,000 km every second.
THAT'S FAST!

So even our solar system is mostly

NOTHING.

Nothing is making my head hurt.

In our galaxy, THE MILKY WAY, there are
over 400,000,000,000 (400 billion) stars.

In the whole Universe, scientists think there are more than
1,000,000,000,000,000,000,000,000 stars.

It's impossible to imagine that number.
Unless you go to a beach...
because a reasonable-sized beach will
contain as many grains of sand as there
are stars in the Universe.

FACT BOX

Stars are giant balls of gas held together by forces of
gravity. The forces are enormous, pulling the gases tighter
and tighter together. Eventually the atoms collapse and
start a process called NUCLEAR FUSION. Fusion is two
atoms joining together and throwing out energy.
Most stars fuse hydrogen into helium.
They radiate this energy as heat and light.

So, to sum up:

You · Stars · The Universe

small · LOTS · BIG!

There are 100 grains of sand drawn in this jar.

Imagine filling it with tiny drawings of grains of sand and keeping count as you draw. You would be amazed at how many it takes to fill the jar.

1, 2, 3, 4, 5, 6...

They are hard to count, Bird. I'd use my fingers and toes but I don't have any!

Our galaxy has tons AND TONS of stars,
but our solar system only has one . . .

THE SUN!

Astronomers know of more than 500 solar systems so far,
and they find new ones every year.

If there are more than 1,000,000,000,000,000,000,000,000 stars,
then there might be more than
1,000,000,000,000,000,000,000,000 solar systems.

Life needs a sun's heat and light to survive,
so a planet like Earth MIGHT be circling one of those stars.
Another important ingredient is LIQUID WATER.
If Earth were closer to the Sun, like Mercury
or Venus, the water would boil.
A bit further away, and we would be an icy ball of rock like Mars.

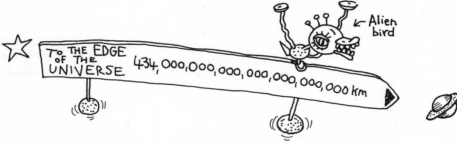

Studying the light that comes from other worlds
tells scientists what gases and elements make up their atmosphere.
Water or oxygen would be good news.
But alien life might not look like we think it's going to . . .

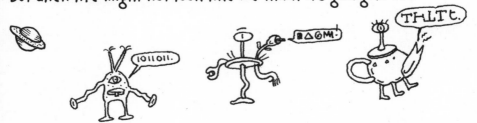

Twinkle, twinkle, little star!
Look up at the stars tonight — they really
do twinkle, but only when they're seen
from Earth. Out in space they just look like
round points of light.

As the starlight comes through the layers
of air and gas that surround our planet,
the light is bent and wobbled.

Soon you will know (almost)

EVERYTHING

there is to know about stars!

But all people USED to know
about them was that they could help us
tell the time at night.
And figure out where we were on Earth,
like a map in the night sky.

For thousands of years we
thought the Earth was flat.
Even 500 years ago we didn't know
that Earth revolved around the Sun.
And after that we thought the Sun was
the centre of the Universe.

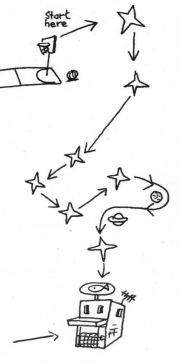

The star map to the centre of
YOUR whole universe.

FLYING VERSUS FRYING

The Sun was born from a GIANT spinning cloud of gas and dust called a NEBULA.
The nebula collapsed, and as it spun faster and faster it flattened into a disc shape, which is what our solar system looks like now.

The Sun formed at the centre and other bits came together around it to become the planets.
Stars have a powerful force called GRAVITY, pulling everything towards them.
So why doesn't Earth get pulled straight in and fried like an egg?

It's because Earth is also travelling FORWARD with a lot of energy, and that forward energy balances out the gravitational force pulling us towards the Sun.

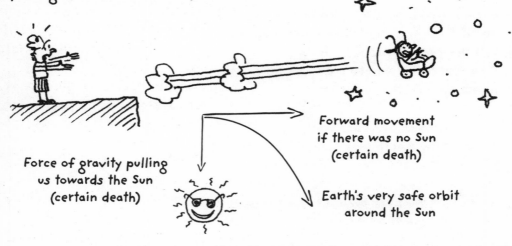

Forward movement if there was no Sun (certain death)

Force of gravity pulling us towards the Sun (certain death)

Earth's very safe orbit around the Sun

If the Sun disappeared, Earth and all the other planets would zoom off in a straight line.
Off we would go into the cold dark NOTHING of space.

COMETS AND ASTEROIDS

We're joined in our journey around the Sun by lots of ASTEROIDS and COMETS.

Comets are made of ice, dust and rock. You can sometimes see their TAIL, which is made of gas and dust.

Halley's Comet is a comet that passes Earth every 75 or 76 years. It's been written about by historians and has appeared in art for thousands of years.

Will I see it again?

You will, I won't.

I will.

Hey, Horse! There's a falling star!

I know, Bird!

Asteroids are lumps of rock that travel around in space. There are billions of them travelling around the Sun in a BELT between Mars and Jupiter.

Some are tiny, but some of the bigger, rounder asteroids get a promotion. They're called DWARF PLANETS.

FACT BOX

When anything from space hits our atmosphere we call it a METEOR. Most meteors burn up and DON'T hit the Earth. We just see a streak of light in the night sky and we call it a falling star. A METEORITE is anything from space that actually hits the Earth's surface. A large meteorite might have been to blame for the extinction of the dinosaurs.

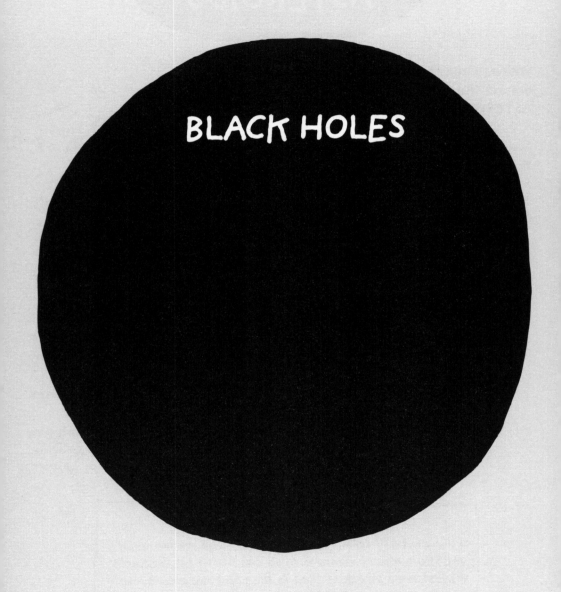

BLACK HOLES

. . . are strange and mysterious.

A brilliant scientist called Albert Einstein
predicted that they existed in 1916.
But astronomers didn't find one until 1971.

A BLACK HOLE is created from the core of a collapsed star.
They can be HUGE or tiny.
They have such powerful gravity that even light gets sucked in.

So you can't SEE a black hole.
Scientists know they are there because
of what happens to objects around them.
Sometimes there is an ACCRETION DISK, a glowing spiral
of gas and dust being sucked towards the hole.

EINSTEIN
AND
BLACK HOLES

MOONS AND PLANETS

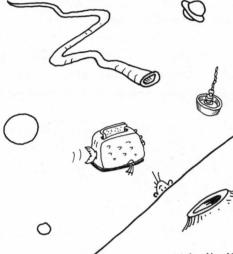

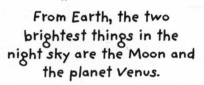

From Earth, the two brightest things in the night sky are the Moon and the planet Venus.

What's the difference between a moon and a planet? MOONS revolve around planets and PLANETS revolve around stars. Easy!

FACT BOX

The Earth is on a slight tilt because a long time ago, when Earth was just a baby planet, something very big hit it and knocked it on an angle. Scientists think that the rubble that was thrown into space from that big hit might have been caught in our orbit and became our moon.

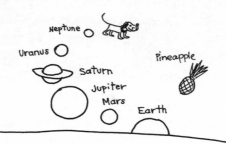

Neptune

Uranus

Saturn

Jupiter

Mars

Earth

Pineapple

Not all moons are dead rocks.
Scientists have evidence that one of Jupiter's moons, Europa,
has a giant saltwater ocean under its icy surface.
It also has a thin oxygen atmosphere.
In lots of ways it's more like Earth than the planet it revolves around.

But ANYTHING floating around in space can get
caught in a planet's orbit and become a moon.

And moons can have things orbiting around them too.

There are eight big planets orbiting the Sun.
But there are other things as well, including all those
asteroids and comets, and dwarf planets like Ceres,
Pluto, Makemake and Eris . . .

Plus loads and loads of cosmic
dust. Yes, that's really a thing!

Our moon is the fifth largest in the Solar System.
It's the only place, other than Earth, that people have walked on.
Because there's no wind or rain the footprints of the astronauts
can still be seen in the dust today.

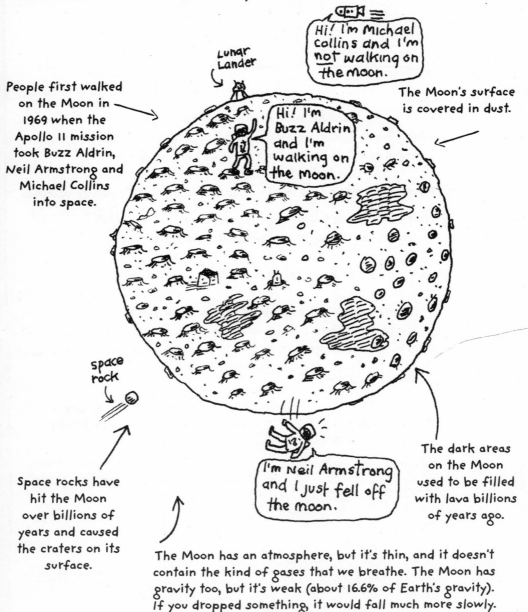

People first walked
on the Moon in
1969 when the
Apollo 11 mission
took Buzz Aldrin,
Neil Armstrong and
Michael Collins
into space.

Lunar
Lander

Hi! I'm Michael
Collins and I'm
not walking on
the moon.

Hi! I'm
Buzz Aldrin
and I'm
walking on
the moon.

The Moon's surface
is covered in dust.

space
rock

Space rocks have
hit the Moon
over billions of
years and caused
the craters on its
surface.

I'm Neil Armstrong
and I just fell off
the moon.

The dark areas
on the Moon
used to be filled
with lava billions
of years ago.

The Moon has an atmosphere, but it's thin, and it doesn't
contain the kind of gases that we breathe. The Moon has
gravity too, but it's weak (about 16.6% of Earth's gravity).
If you dropped something, it would fall much more slowly.
You would weigh about one sixth of what you weigh on Earth.

The Moon takes 27.3 days to travel around the Earth.

It's also spinning and that takes 27.3 days too.

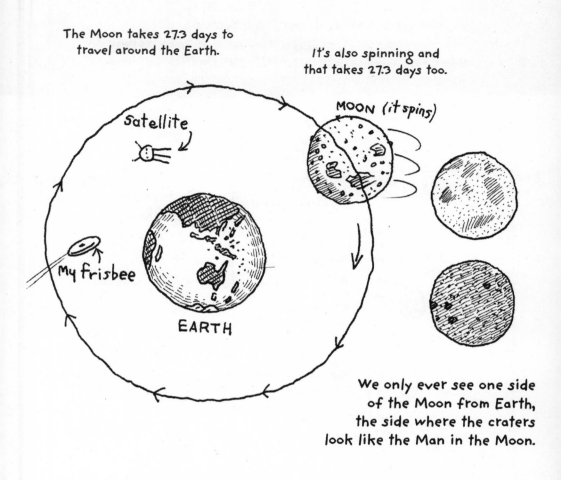

MOON (it spins)

satellite

My frisbee

EARTH

We only ever see one side of the Moon from Earth, the side where the craters look like the Man in the Moon.

The changes to the Moon that we see from Earth are just the Sun lighting up different areas of the Moon from where we're standing. It takes about 29.5 days to go through the whole cycle, a bit longer than the Moon's actual journey around the Earth.

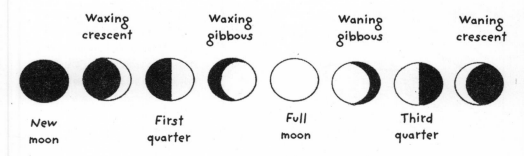

Waxing crescent

Waxing gibbous

Waning gibbous

Waning crescent

New moon

First quarter

Full moon

Third quarter

OUR SOLAR SYSTEM

We feel like we're standing still here on Earth, but like the Moon
we're always on the move. Our planet is turning,
and the time it takes to do that is called a DAY.

Newly discovered
planet Cupcake.
Delicious!

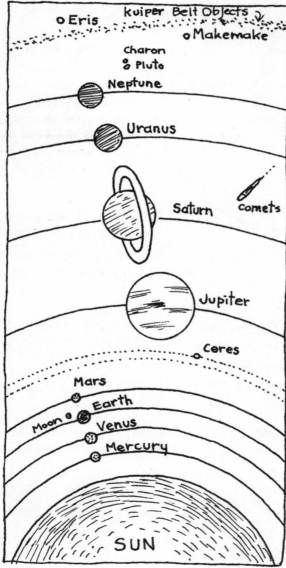

Kuiper Belt Objects

o Eris

o Makemake

Charon
♀ Pluto

Neptune

Uranus

Saturn   comets

Jupiter

Ceres

Mars

Moon ●   Earth

Venus

Mercury

SUN

The gassy planets are
further from the Sun
and the rocky ones
are closer.

I rule this
cupcake
planet?!

The Sun is a YELLOW
DWARF star.
The gassy surface is called
the PHOTOSPHERE.

The outer layer of the Sun's
atmosphere is called the
CORONA. You can only see
it during a SOLAR ECLIPSE,
when the Moon is between
us and the Sun.

At the same time, our turning planet is slowly moving around the Sun. Not all planets take the same amount of time to circle their star, and some planets even circle TWO stars, but at the moment we take 365.25 days to go around ours. We call the journey ONE YEAR.

NEPTUNE

4,500 million km from the Sun. A similar size to Uranus. Made of gas and ice with thin rings made of ice and dust. Has 14 moons. Forget living here.

URANUS

2,900 million km from the Sun. Four times bigger than Earth. The coldest planet. Made of gas and ice. Has 27 moons. The icy atmosphere gives it a pale blue colour. Not pleasant for humans.

 ←Ring

SATURN

1,400 million km from the Sun. Big and gassy like Jupiter. Has 'rings' made of chunks of ice and dust, and 32 moons. Don't even visit.

Red spot

JUPITER

780 million km from the Sun. The biggest planet. Has 79 moons, giant 'rings' made of dust, and a storm that can be seen from space that has lasted for 350 years. All hot gas and NO FUN.

MARS

230 million km from the Sun. Half the size of Earth. The second smallest planet. Has two moons. Its surface has an orange/red colour, but it's COLD. Don't live here.

EARTH

150 million km from the Sun. A good place to live.

VENUS

110 million km from the Sun. As big as Earth, but very hot. Has no moons and is covered in clouds of sulphuric acid. Ouch.

MERCURY

58 million km from the Sun. Doesn't have any moons and is the smallest planet. Very hot and the closest to the Sun, but not the hottest planet!

FACT BOX

Space is completely silent because sound is only produced when something vibrates. On Earth, air molecules carry vibration to your ears. Light and radio waves can travel in the big fat NOTHING of space, but sound can't. That's why astronauts use radios to communicate.

It was about 4.5 billion years ago that the Sun was created from a cloud of dust and gas. That seems like a LONG TIME AGO. And it is!

But WAY WAY back, 14 BILLION YEARS AGO . . .

It is very BIG, this BANG.!!

THE BIG BANG CREATED ATOMS

ATOMS make up everything that exists. EVERYTHING!

Hydrogen Atom (Very simple)

Atoms combine to become MOLECULES, which combine to become

EVERYTHING.

Atoms look like this, with a heavy bit in the middle (the NUCLEUS) and tiny ELECTRONS flying around outside.

Electron

Nucleus

But an atom is mostly NOTHING.
And you are made of atoms so YOU are mostly NOTHING.
And all the planets, moons and stars are made of atoms, so they are mostly

NOTHING!

It's hard to believe, but it's true.

Helium Atom

Carbon Atom

The dark bits in the middle are the protons. The light bits are the neutrons.

FACT BOX

Atoms are the building blocks of the Universe. Atoms are incredibly tiny, but they're made up of even tinier things called SUB-ATOMIC PARTICLES (PROTONS and NEUTRONS in the nucleus, plus electrons). Even sub-atomic particles are made of smaller things, called HADRONS and QUARKS. They were too small to draw. Does it get even smaller than that? We just don't know.

YOU are small compared to a

STAR

Star ↘

But compared to an ant you are

BIG

You →

← Ant

UNLESS, of course, the ant is a

GIANT ANT.

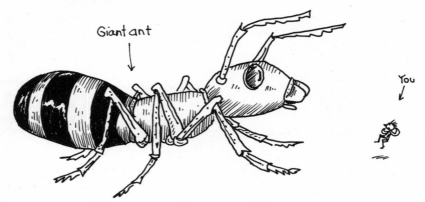

Giant ant ↓

You ↓

BUT even the teeniest tiniest ant is

HUGE

compared to a micro-animal
like a tardigrade.
They are only 0.5 mm long,
even when they're fully grown.

Actual size

Tardigrade

NOT actual
size.

Scientists keep finding
smaller
and smaller
living things.

They have found BACTERIA
that is only five thousandth of
a millimetre long.

VIRUSES, like the flu or measles or
the coronavirus, are even tinier.

Viruses are so small
you can't see them
without a microscope.

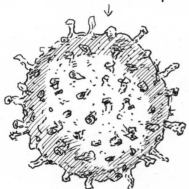

Most scientists don't consider
viruses to be properly alive.
They can't do ANYTHING without
a HOST. Sometimes that's us!
The host helps them grow and
copy themselves and spread.

FACT BOX

We can measure distances in space by how many
LIGHT YEARS things are away. One light year is about
9.46 trillion kilometres. It's the distance light travels
in a vacuum in one Earth year. Its symbol is ly.

REACH FOR THE STARS

People have been looking up at the stars for a long time . . . but we've only just started to take baby steps out into space.

Sputnik 1
1957

We put the first spacecraft into Earth's orbit in 1957.

It was called Sputnik 1.

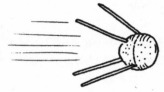

Damn! Dried food again!

Sputnik 2
1957

Later that year Sputnik 2 took the first animal into orbit. She was NOT a cat. She was a dog called Laika. Sadly she didn't get to come home again.

HOW WE'D LIKE TO REMEMBER LAIKA THE SPACE DOG
(The real story is not so sweet)

CCCP

Yuri Gagarin
1961

The first human to journey into outer space was Yuri Gagarin. In 1961, he went around the Earth . . . and landed safely again.

In 1965, Alexei Leonov
took the first SPACE WALK.

He wouldn't have been able
to survive the radiation and extreme
temperatures of space without
his suit for protection.

Space flight is DANGEROUS.
There's a Fallen Astronaut memorial
on the Moon that includes people
who have died in space.

But, don't worry, Alexei came back.

First humans
walk on the Moon
1969

In 1969, the first humans
to travel to the Moon,
walked on its surface.

They came back safely too!

Lots of animals have been sent to space, especially
in the 1940s and 1950s. Not a lot of them survived.

The first mammal in space,
a monkey called Albert II,
got there 12 years before
Yuri Gagarin did.

(R.I.P. Albert.)

Albert II in his
horrifying
space harness.

Thinking about how

BIG

the Universe is
can make you feel
really tiny.

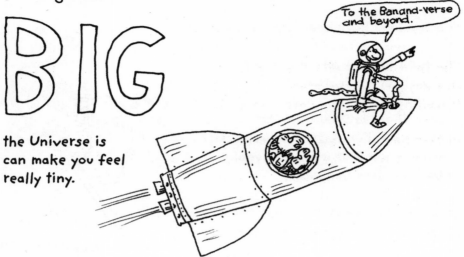

 YOUR
WHOLE GALAXY

But did you know that you can live in space right now?
For about 20 years, astronauts have been
able to live and work on the INTERNATIONAL SPACE STATION.

It travels around the Earth 15.5 times a day.

The twin spacecrafts Voyager 1
and Voyager 2 have been
travelling away from Earth since 1977.

In that time they've already made it
past the edge of the Solar System.
They're in interstellar space
outside our HELIOSPHERE,
which is what we call
the part of space around the Sun.

Voyager looks
a bit like this.

The nearest solar system to ours is ALPHA CENTAURI.
It has three stars.
But we won't be popping in any time soon.
It's over 41 trillion kilometres away.

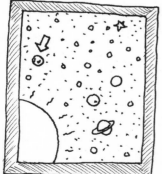

There are no people on Voyager 1 and Voyager 2,
but the sensors are still sending information back.

Voyager 1 recently took the first picture
of our heliosphere from the outside.

And that's

SOMETHING!

HOME, SWEET HOME

2

YOUR PLANET
EARTH

The third planet from the Sun is our

HOME, SWEET HOME!

It's the only place in the Solar System, maybe the only place in the Universe, we can survive.

AUSTRALIA

ANTARCTICA

ASIA

AFRICA

EUROPE

NORTH AMERICA

SOUTH AMERICA

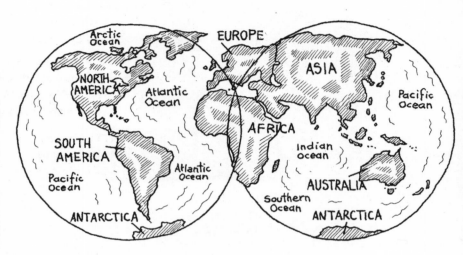

We live on continents and islands.
A CONTINENT might be a big island surrounded by water, like Australia, or joined to another continent by a little bridge of land, like the Americas, or completely joined up to another continent, like Europe and Asia.

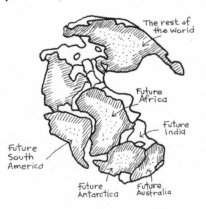

PANGAEA

The world map hasn't always looked like this. From about 335 million to about 175 million years ago, the Earth had just one big continent, called PANGAEA.

That's not the first time lots of continents joined up and broke apart again. And it won't be the last.

Life evolved in Earth's water, using the Sun's energy and breathing Earth's air. All life we know of is mostly made up of carbon, hydrogen, nitrogen and oxygen atoms. Life is awesome. But non-living things are just as interesting and complex.

WHAT IS THE EARTH MADE OF?

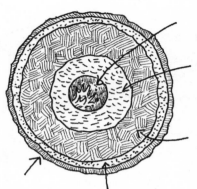

INNER CORE A solid ball of iron and nickel. It's nearly 6,000°C. That's SUPER HOT!

OUTER CORE A very hot layer of molten iron and nickel. It's about 3,000 km down . . . Dig a HUGE hole and toast some marshmallows.

LOWER MANTLE A hot, sometimes liquid, layer of rock. Still a bit of a dig to get there.

CRUST A thin layer, 5–75 km thick. This is the ground we walk, live, play and build on.

UPPER MANTLE A solid rock, cooler than the lower mantle. Together, both mantles are about 3,000 km thick.

Don't chomp into the Earth's core, Horse. We'll explode!!

CHOMP! CHOMP!

WHAT SHOULD THE EARTH BE MADE OF?

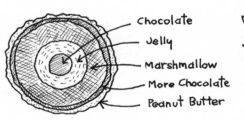

Chocolate

Jelly

Marshmallow

More Chocolate

Peanut Butter

FACT BOX

What does the Earth weigh? WEIGHT is actually how much matter you're made of (called your MASS) multiplied by the force of Earth's gravity. Your mass is always the same, but you would weigh LESS on the Moon because the Moon has weaker gravity. We can't pop the Earth on a giant set of scales. But if you could, its weight would be about 5,900,000,000,000,000,000,000,000 kg.

NATURAL OR NATURAL DISASTER?

The Earth's crust is a giant jigsaw puzzle.

The pieces are called TECTONIC PLATES. That's how continents can break up and move around. The cracks between the plates are called FAULT LINES.

The most famous fault line is the Ring of Fire. Over 75% of Earth's active volcanoes are on the Ring of Fire. That's 452 volcanoes.

In 1883, Krakatoa in Indonesia erupted, destroying most of the island. You could hear the explosions from Australia. It was one of the most deadly volcanic events in history.

When plates move, EARTHQUAKES happen at the fault lines and VOLCANOES erupt. The ground shakes and can split apart. If that happens underwater, huge waves are created. They cause destruction and flooding when they hit the shore. That's a TSUNAMI!

Earthquakes can destroy entire cities, break roads and cause accidents.

They are sometimes caused by boiling rock trying to break through to the Earth's surface and sometimes by the movement of tectonic plates.

Living on a changing planet can be dangerous. But some of the big events that we think of as natural disasters are also the events that created the world around us. Volcanoes and earthquakes are scary, but they also created Earth's wonderful mountains, hills and valleys.

Sometimes a big bulge of magma pushes the ground up into a mountain but doesn't erupt.

A bulge creates a DOME MOUNTAIN

magma

Hawaii's islands are the peaks of a giant underwater mountain range that was created when boiling hot rock erupted and piled up. They're still erupting.

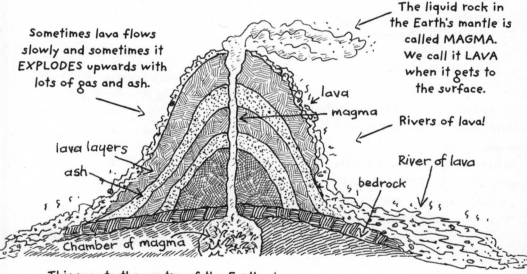

Sometimes lava flows slowly and sometimes it EXPLODES upwards with lots of gas and ash.

The liquid rock in the Earth's mantle is called MAGMA. We call it LAVA when it gets to the surface.

lava

magma

Rivers of lava!

lava layers

ash

River of lava

bedrock

Chamber of magma

This way to the centre of the Earth.

FACT BOX

Earthquakes are the DEADLIEST of all natural disasters. One of the worst in recent times was the 2004 Indian Ocean earthquake and tsunami. Up to 280,000 people in 14 countries were killed and in Indonesia the waves reached 30 m high. That's about the height of an 8-storey building.

ROCK ON!

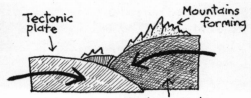

Tectonic plate

Mountains forming

Tectonic Plate

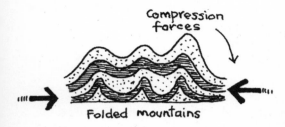

Compression forces

Folded mountains

Most of our biggest mountains were created when tectonic plates hit each other and the ground was pushed up.

Like when India crashed into Asia in slow motion creating the Himalayas (it took millions of years). That creates a FOLDED MOUNTAIN like Mount Everest.

Fault-block mountains

Mountains can also be created when fault lines pull apart, pushing up and dropping big pillars of rock. That creates a FAULT-BLOCK MOUNTAIN.

It's just erosion, Horse.

Mountains are MASSIVE, but the rocks from even the biggest mountain can be broken down to tiny grains of sand by EROSION.

FACT BOX

Sometimes mountains are created when giant glaciers wear the surrounding ground away or when the ground is worn away by rivers, creating a valley. Water is very powerful. When rock is broken down into tiny pieces by water, wind, ice or landslides it's called EROSION.

Rocks and sand are both made up of molecules called MINERALS. When sand is pushed together under pressure, it can turn back into rock, called SANDSTONE.

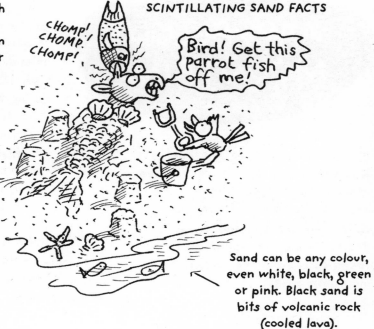

CHOMP! CHOMP! CHOMP!

Bird! Get this parrot fish off me!

Some sand ISN'T eroded rock. Fine white sand is made from the poo of parrotfish! They eat algae off rocks and coral, and they poop out the bit they can't digest.

Sand can be any colour, even white, black, green or pink. Black sand is bits of volcanic rock (cooled lava).

Sand isn't always formed near the beach. Rivers carry it to the sea and the ocean erodes it even more. Water can even create caves by dissolving rock called LIMESTONE or tunnelling into ice.

THINGS TO KNOW ABOUT CAVES

Clouds can form in large caves and create underground weather.

Giant sinkholes can let in light so there can be a forest growing underground.

STALACTITES grow from the roof when dripping water leaves minerals behind.

The largest cave in the world is the Hang Son Doong cave, in Vietnam.

STALAGMITES are formed when water with minerals in it drips onto the floor.

It's SO BIG you could fit heaps of 40-storey skyscrapers in there.

MARVELLOUS MOUNTAINS

The highest point above sea level is the top of Mount Everest in the Himalayas. At 8,848 m high, it's just rocks and ice up there. The air is too thin to breathe. Nothing can survive there for long.

But measuring above sea level is just measuring the bit you can see. Mauna Kea in Hawaii is 10,210 m from the base to the summit. About half of it is under the Pacific Ocean, though. So it technically wins the 'tallest mountain' prize.

Mountain goat →

The top of a mountain is called the SUMMIT.

Is that a Yeti?

Rows of mountains are called RANGES.

To live on a mountain you need to eat small plants that can grow in the rocky ground, enjoy the cold and be good at climbing slippery rocks. Mountain goats live on mountains. Monkeys do NOT.

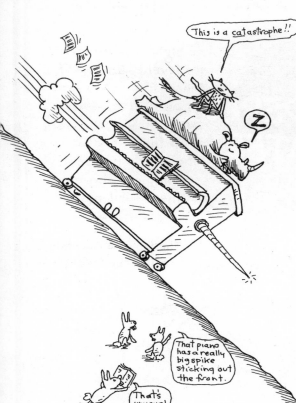

An AVALANCHE is when a huge chunk of snow comes loose from the mountainside and slides down. It collects more snow and rocks and ice as it goes faster and gets more powerful.

The most deadly avalanche was caused by the Great Peruvian Earthquake in 1970. It killed 20,000 people.

A rhino-lanche is when a piano-playing rhino has a nap at the top of a hill and forgets to put the brakes on.

An avalanche can break your bones or bury you so you die from the cold or suffocate.

A rhino-lanche is EVEN MORE DEADLY, but fortunately they are quite rare.

FACT BOX

The Earth isn't perfectly round. It's a bit fatter across the middle than it is between the poles. That fat bit is known as the EQUATOR. The difference is more than twice the height of the highest mountain or deepest ocean trench. If you were measuring the highest mountain peak from the centre of the Earth, Mount Chimborazo in Ecuador would beat Mount Everest because it sits right on the bulge. But that's like standing on a rock to have your height measured.

WONDERFUL WATER

Only one-third of the surface of the Earth is LAND.

So that means lots and LOTS and LOTS AND LOTS of the Earth is covered by water.

An island

These are also islands. Not noses. I can't believe you would even SUGGEST they look like noses. Grow up!

When Earth was a boiling baby planet, there wasn't any liquid water. But when things cooled down, rain started to fall . . .
and fall . . .
and fall . . .

Eventually the valleys filled up and became oceans.

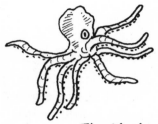

All sea water was fresh until salt was washed down by the rivers. The ocean is still less salty in rainy places, and there are lots of lakes in dry parts of the world that are even saltier than sea water.

The Mariana Trench in the Pacific Ocean is deeper than Mount Everest is high. After about 1,000 m down, it's pitch black and the water is nearly freezing. But some creatures have evolved so they can survive. There's a fish with a see-through head, and one with a glowing light suspended just above its mouth.

FACT BOX

The oceans are filled with animals that have evolved to deal with salt. But it takes so much water from OUR bodies to get rid of salt that drinking sea water is deadly. Humans need to be about 60% fresh water to survive so we can't afford to lose too much. Some land animals are 90% water, which is almost as much as plants.

RIVERS AND LAKES AND UNDERGROUND WATER

When you step on liquid water, the molecules move apart and you SINK.

platypus

Fish

pond skater

But even huge boats can FLOAT if they weigh less than the same amount of water would weigh. Submarines increase their BUOYANCY by filling their tanks with air. And make themselves heavier by filling them with water.

YABBY

frog

A RIVER is just a big long ditch that water flows down. The Nile (6,500 km) and the Amazon (6,400 km) are the longest rivers in the world. Australia's Murray (2,500 km) is pretty long too. 90% of the frozen water in the world is in Antarctica. A GLACIER is a slow-moving river of ice.

Tadpoles

Tortoise

Eel

Lucky us! Earth has lots of lovely water. So why does everyone worry about droughts? Because only about 2.5% of the water on Earth is fresh water. The rest is salty. And of that fresh water, most of it is underground or ice so we rely on rain and snow and dew to survive.

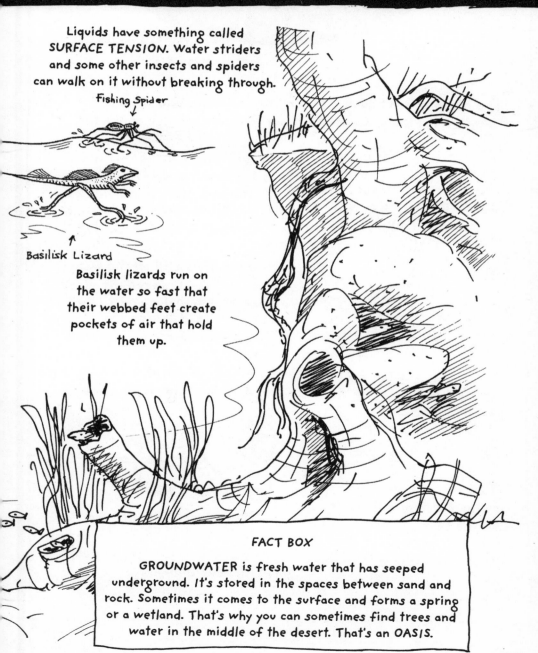

Liquids have something called SURFACE TENSION. Water striders and some other insects and spiders can walk on it without breaking through.

Fishing Spider

Basilisk Lizard

Basilisk lizards run on the water so fast that their webbed feet create pockets of air that hold them up.

FACT BOX

GROUNDWATER is fresh water that has seeped underground. It's stored in the spaces between sand and rock. Sometimes it comes to the surface and forms a spring or a wetland. That's why you can sometimes find trees and water in the middle of the desert. That's an OASIS.

WATER AND THE MOON

The Moon doesn't have a single drop of water and it's about 380,000 km away. So what's it got to do with water on Earth?

You might have noticed that if you go to the beach at different times, the water will be further up or lower down the sand. That's a high or low TIDE.

The Earth's gravity stops all the water (and everything else) from floating away into space.

I'm the Moon and I have gravity!

But the Moon has gravity too.

That force is pulling at the Earth and its water all the time.

That's what causes the tides.

There's no evidence that the Full Moon can affect animal's behaviour. But lots of people believe it anyway.

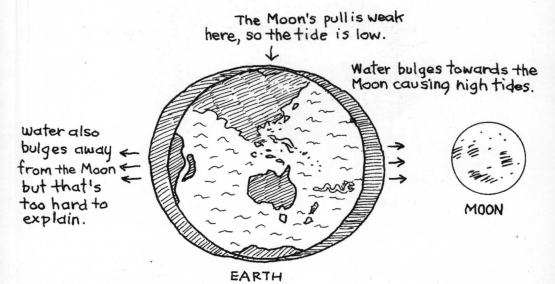

The Moon's pull is weak here, so the tide is low.

Water bulges towards the Moon causing high tides.

water also bulges away from the Moon but that's too hard to explain.

MOON

EARTH

When the Moon looks full,
it means that the Earth is between the Sun and the Moon.

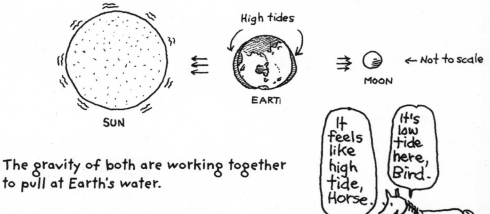

High tides

Not to scale

SUN

EARTI

MOON

It feels like high tide, Horse.

It's low tide here, Bird.

The gravity of both are working together to pull at Earth's water.

Then you see very high tides.

FACT BOX

The same tidal pull is working on your glass of cordial as well, but you won't notice it. Lakes and rivers aren't usually big enough to have tides that you can see, but the larger the amount of water, the more movement there will be.

USE THE POWER OF THE FORCE

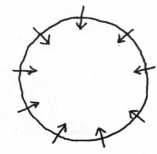

Earth's gravity pulls everything in towards the centre.

A guy called Isaac Newton apparently came up with the THEORY OF GRAVITY when something fell out of a tree and hit him on the head.
Thankfully it was an apple, not a horse.

Hey, Bird. Look at me, I'm floating. It's YTIVARG!!

If you let go of a horse, Earth's gravity makes the horse drop down.
In space, a long way from Earth the horse would float because there is no gravity.

He was already a brilliant scientist, though, so he might already have had some idea. His book, published in 1687, changed science forever.

THE FORCE OF GRAVITY exists between everything in the Universe.

It's what gives things weight when they're on Earth and makes objects fall.

It was my idea and Newton gets all the glory.

Massive things like planets have more gravitational pull than little things, but gravity DOESN'T pull heavier things down any faster than light things.

Gravity isn't the only force at work on Earth.

What if you dropped a hammer and a feather?
Which would land first?

On Earth the hammer
would hit first because
air molecules are getting
in the way of both
objects as they fall.
The hammer has more
mass so it's better at
knocking air molecules
out of the way.

In space, where there's no air, they would travel at the same speed.
The Apollo 15 moonwalk tried this out and took a film.
You can look it up online.

Anything that moves or slows or stops
can only do that because of
THE FORCE OF FRICTION.

Friction is created when two surfaces
rub against each other.

KLANK!!

Stop rubbing,
Bird, I think
I smell my
bottom burning!

Rub!

Rub!

Rub!

Friction between surfaces
can even make fire.
That's why rubbing two sticks
together creates a spark.

Smooth things create
less friction than rough things.

If there's friction
is there non-friction
as well?

The air resistance that slows the feather
more than the hammer is a type of friction.
It's also called DRAG.

Another force we rely on is MAGNETIC FORCE.
Every magnet has a south pole and a north pole.

South poles repel each other.

North poles repel each other.

North and south poles attract
each other.

Magnetism and electricity are very closely related.
Both are caused by the movement of electrons.
Remember electrons, the particles that orbit around atoms?

Magnets have the power to attract some metals.
And the magnets we use are MADE of metal.

But the biggest magnet in our world is the planet itself.
That's right! Earth is a GIANT MAGNET.
That's why we have a north pole
and a south pole.

Yee-Haw!

MIND BLOWN!

Earth ISN'T a very POWERFUL magnet.

But our magnetic field protects us from SOLAR WIND.
That's particles from the Sun that would destroy our atmosphere.

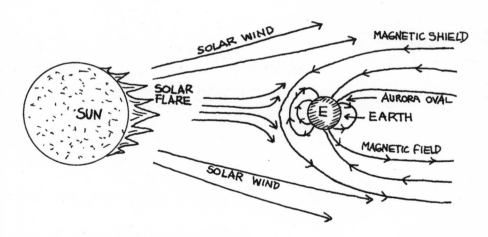

SOLAR WIND   MAGNETIC SHIELD

SOLAR
FLARE   AURORA OVAL
SUN   E   EARTH
MAGNETIC FIELD

SOLAR WIND

Solar wind causes amazing, colourful lights in the sky at the poles.
A solar storm can even make technology fail and cause power blackouts.

That sounds like science fiction
but it's REAL SCIENCE.

Our ATMOSPHERE keeps the air in,
stops the Sun's radiation from frying us and meteors from hitting us.
Thank goodness gravity stops it from floating off into space,
and Earth's magnetic field keeps it safe.
The air we breathe is mainly 78% nitrogen and 20% oxygen.
It's the oxygen bit that we need.
Oxygen keeps us alive.

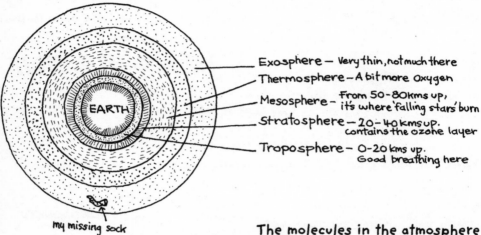

Exosphere — Very thin, not much there
Thermosphere — A bit more oxygen
Mesosphere — From 50-80kms up, it's where 'falling stars' burn
Stratosphere — 20-40kms up. Contains the ozone layer
Troposphere — 0-20kms up. Good breathing here

my missing sock

The molecules in the atmosphere
wobble light to make the stars look twinkly.
They also scatter sunlight into colours.

All the colours we can see are contained in light.
Air molecules scatter the blue bits of the light
more easily than the other colours.

That's why the daytime sky normally looks blue.

But when the Sun is on the horizon,
the light has to travel through more atmosphere to get to your eyes.
By then all the blue has been scattered away so you get a chance
to see the beautiful reds, yellows, oranges and pinks.
And that's sunset and sunrise.

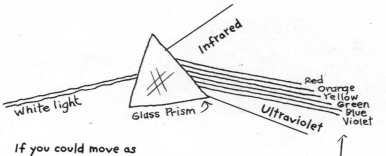

Infrared

White light

Glass Prism ↗

Ultraviolet

Red
Orange
Yellow
Green
Blue
Violet

All colours are contained in white light. Each colour has a different WAVELENGTH.

If you could move as fast as light, you could travel around the Earth 7.5 times in one second.

Light is bent by a glass prism to show us all the colours we can see. Different gases, liquids and solids all scatter the wavelengths differently or absorb some of them. That's why things are different colours.

When sunlight passes through water droplets in our atmosphere we see the colours as a RAINBOW. But the light we can see is just a small part of the ELECTROMAGNETIC SPECTRUM.

Before the red side of the spectrum there are longer wavelengths we can't see called INFRARED radiation. That's what makes sunlight warm.

After the violet side of the spectrum is invisible ULTRAVIOLET (UV) light. That's what causes sunlight to BURN.

Reflection at work

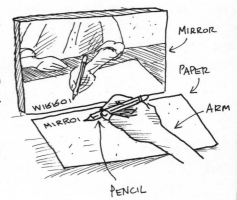

MIRROR

PAPER

ARM

MIRROI

PENCIL

FACT BOX

You can only see this book because light is hitting it and bouncing back into your eyes. SHADOWS are just areas where the light has been blocked. That's why your shadow is the same shape as you. And a REFLECTION happens when light bounces off a shiny surface like a mirror or water.

AIR POLLUTION

Sorry!

DANGER!
FART JOKE

Oops!

When harmful gases are pumped
into the air we breathe, it's bad for our health.
But some pollution is bad for the WHOLE PLANET.

Some gases, called GREENHOUSE GASES,
trap the heat from sunlight inside our atmosphere.
That makes the temperature warmer,
and causes CLIMATE CHANGE.

Climate change makes some areas
unliveable for animals and plants.
It causes glaciers to melt
and water levels to rise.
It means more destructive droughts,
storms, fires and floods.

That's not
Carbon dioxide,
Bird.

Carbon dioxide is a greenhouse gas.

Lots of things produce it.
But burning things called FOSSIL FUELS
creates MASSIVE amounts.
And humans keep cutting down the forests
that turn carbon dioxide into oxygen.

Excellent one, Mabel!

What's that got to do with popping off?
People farm a LOT of cows, and their
farting and burping creates LOADS
of another powerful greenhouse gas.

METHANE! Talk about silent but deadly . . .

50

We burn fuel through a chemical reaction called COMBUSTION.

Things can't just burst into flame. They have to be heated until a gas is produced.

The gas reacts with oxygen in the air and turns chemical energy into heat and light energy.

You can stop combustion by removing the fuel, the oxygen or the heat.

Smoke is made of the new molecules formed by combustion, and the leftover bits from the fuel, like ash and water vapour.

COOKING POT

FIRE

Different fuels release different gases and burn with differently coloured FLAMES that are different temperatures.

WOOD

You can't use water on an oil fire because the fire will be hotter than the boiling point of water. The water will turn to steam and throw boiling oil everywhere.

FACT BOX

OZONE is made up of three oxygen atoms. The ozone layer protects us from dangerous ultraviolet B radiation from the Sun. In the 1970s, scientists realised that certain chemicals made by humans were destroying the ozone. The good news is that people across the world listened and banned those chemicals. And the ozone layer is recovering.

Plants PHOTOSYNTHESISE during the day.

They use the energy from sunlight
to turn water and carbon dioxide into
a different kind of energy.
They use that energy to grow.

Plants release
oxygen back into
the air.

Plants absorb water
through their roots and
carbon dioxide from the
air through their leaves.

Carbon dioxide + water + the Sun's energy =
glucose energy + oxygen

It's not just trees and plants on land.
Millions of teeny tiny plants
that live in the ocean,
produce HUGE amounts of lovely oxygen.

Not
oxygen

Oxygen
released

Oxygen

Phytoplankton and algae

Oxygen

THE CARBON CYCLE

Life breathes.
Even plants take in oxygen through tiny air holes at night.
Living things need the oxygen to make energy
in a process called RESPIRATION.

When animals and plants
use oxygen to create energy
in their bodies
they produce carbon dioxide.

Animals breathe it out.

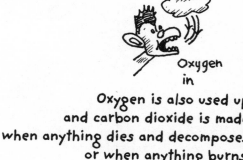

Plant

Carbon
dioxide
in

Oxygen
out

Oxygen
in

Oxygen is also used up
and carbon dioxide is made
when anything dies and decomposes
or when anything burns.
That's the CARBON CYCLE.

Even I breathe like that.
We're the same!

FACT BOX

Even fish use oxygen. The water comes in through their
mouth, and their gills take out oxygen from the water
using lots of tiny blood vessels (water is made up of two
hydrogen atoms and one oxygen atom). Some fish, like
mudskippers, can also breathe air and survive out of water.
Frogs have gills when they are tadpoles
and lungs when they are frogs.

THE WATER CYCLE

A water molecule looks like this.

But one tiny drop of pure water is actually made up of BILLIONS of water molecules.

And those molecules keep moving around the Earth in different STATES.

HERE'S HOW IT WORKS

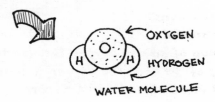

OXYGEN

HYDROGEN

WATER MOLECULE

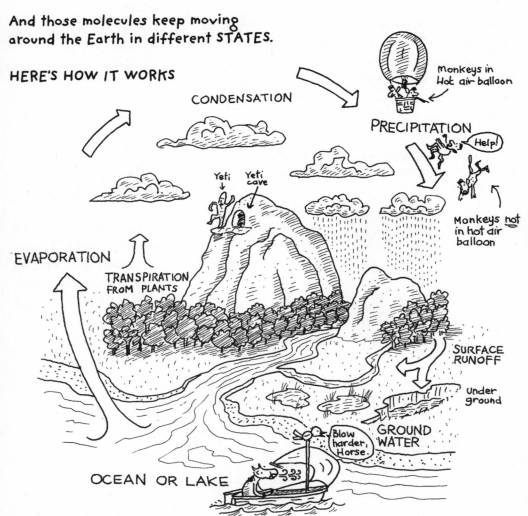

CONDENSATION

Monkeys in hot air balloon

PRECIPITATION

Help!

Monkeys not in hot air balloon

Yeti

Yeti cave

EVAPORATION

TRANSPIRATION FROM PLANTS

SURFACE RUNOFF

Under ground

GROUND WATER

Blow harder, Horse.

OCEAN OR LAKE

Water is pretty special. On Earth it easily becomes a liquid, a solid and a gas. All molecules can change state like that, but usually it would take a huge temperature or pressure change, and humans couldn't survive either of those things.

What are clouds? The air around us is made up of small amounts of WATER VAPOUR.

When water vapour cools to form water droplets and tiny ice crystals, then you start to see clouds.

CIRRUS

Big high windswept clouds

CIRRO-CUMULUS

Rows of smaller lumpy clouds

CUMULUS

Big mountainous lumpy clouds

STRATO-CUMULUS

Long bands of small lumpy clouds

STRATUS

Thin low lumpy but wispy clouds

So the water molecules you're drinking today are exactly the same water molecules that the dinosaurs drank.

TERRY DACTYL

Bleagh! This water tastes of pterodactyl!

FACT BOX

To change the state of water you just need to add or take away heat energy. When you add heat to frozen water, the molecules move faster and can't hold on to each other anymore. When you boil water, they can't hold on to each other at all! When you take heat away, they slow down and hold on very tight again to become ice.

WILD WEATHER

TORNADOES and CYCLONES (also called hurricanes and typhoons) are storms that spin around and around at amazing speeds. Tornadoes form under thunderstorms on land, but cyclones are HUGE and form over water in warm places.

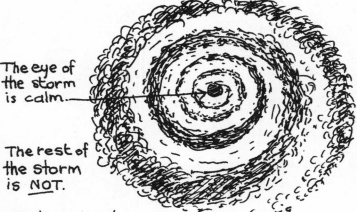

The eye of the storm is calm.

The rest of the storm is NOT.

Wind can reach up to 300km/hr.

We name storms so people can remember them and talk about them more easily.

Cyclone Monkey

Cyclone Tracy was the second smallest cyclone ever recorded. It still killed 71 people and destroyed Darwin on Christmas Day, 1974.

The Bhola cyclone killed approximately 500,000 people in Bangladesh in 1970. It's one of the deadliest natural disasters ever. Cyclones can cause SEA SURGES of up to 10 m. They can wipe out whole islands. And flooding causes destruction, mudslides and disease.

We appreciate a bit of rain and a nice breeze — but hail and strong winds and too much rain can mean destruction and flooding. Not enough rain can mean drought and out-of-control bushfires.

BUSHFIRES are out-of-control fires.
They travel EVEN FASTER when they burn up a hill.
They can be caused by lightning,
but they can also MAKE their own lightning.

A change in the wind can change the direction of a bushfire. And a strong wind will push more oxygen into the fire and make it worse.

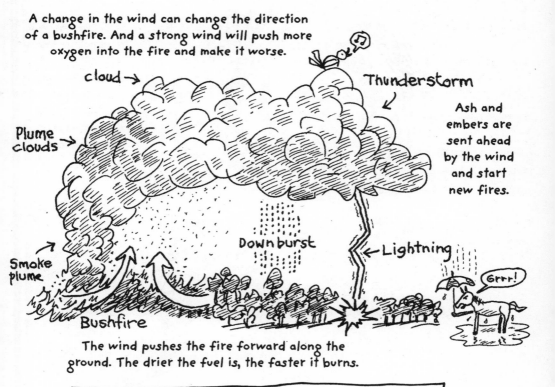

cloud →

Thunderstorm

Plume clouds →

Ash and embers are sent ahead by the wind and start new fires.

Downburst

Smoke plume

←Lightning

Grrr!

Bushfire

The wind pushes the fire forward along the ground. The drier the fuel is, the faster it burns.

FACT BOX

Clouds that form above a big bushfire because of super-heated, super-dry air are called PYROCUMULONIMBUS CLOUDS. They can sometimes cause rain (good news) although usually not on the fire. More often they cause wild winds, dry lightning and fire tornadoes (VERY bad news).

ELECTRICAL ENERGY IS EVERYWHERE

Electricity is in the sky as lightning and in our bodies powering us.

Remember how atoms make up EVERYTHING that exists?

ELECTRICITY is the flow of electrons between atoms. You can easily move electrons by rubbing two things together.

But atoms prefer to have an equal number of electrons and protons.

When something has too many electrons they will leave it with a SPARK and a ZAP as soon as it touches something else.

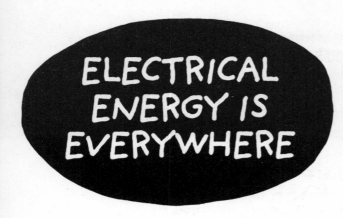

Electron

Nucleus

Electrons are not heavy and they have a negative charge.

The nucleus is made of positively charged protons (which are heavy) and neutral neutrons.

RUB RUB RUB

Monkey 1 rubs bottom on carpet creating a negative charge.

ZAP!

Monkey 1 touches Monkey 2 giving him a shock!

Meanwhile Monkey 3 runs away.

If you slide your SHOES (not your bum, please) along the carpet you can move some electrons, make a tiny charge and ZAP your friend.

That's STATIC ELECTRICITY.

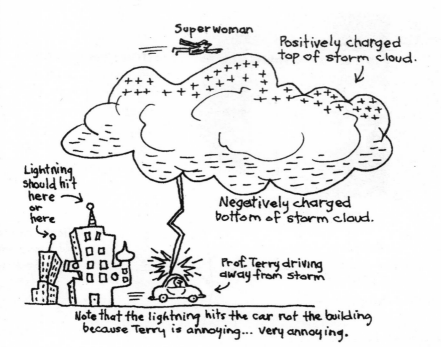

Superwoman

Positively charged
top of storm cloud.

+ + +
+ + + + + + + +
+ + + + + + + + +
+ + + + + + + + +

Lightning
should hit
here →
or
here →

Negatively charged
bottom of storm cloud.

Prof. Terry driving
away from storm ←

Note that the lightning hits the car not the building
because Terry is annoying... very annoying.

LIGHTNING is a type of static electricity.
When lots of dust and ice crystals rub together
in a thunder cloud, electrons build up.
They have to go somewhere.

They flow through the air in a giant spark.
The air gets heated up.
THUNDER is the sound of the air expanding
in a big CRACK.

You hear the thunder AFTER you
see the lightning because light
travels faster than sound.

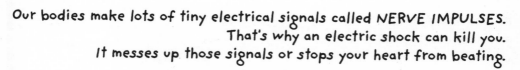

Our bodies make lots of tiny electrical signals called NERVE IMPULSES.
That's why an electric shock can kill you.
It messes up those signals or stops your heart from beating.

Right now, your cells are passing a teensy electrical charge from your
brain saying, 'STOP PICKING YOUR NOSE AND TURN THE PAGE!'

The WEATHER changes with the SEASONS,
but not in the same way everywhere, and not all cultures have four.

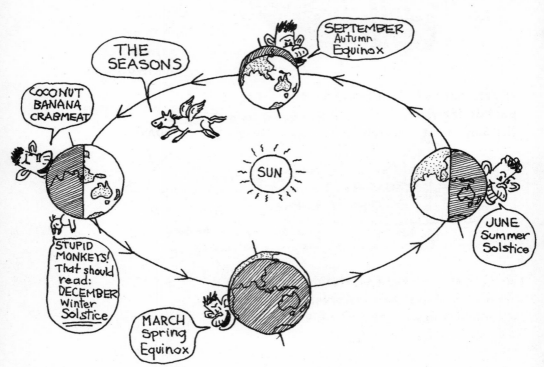

Because Earth got knocked on an angle when it was just a baby planet,
it's on a slight tilt. But the north pole is always pointing the same way.

The amount of sunlight your home gets
is a bit different on each day of the year.

Sunrise and sunset are at
different times too.

The days are
longer in summer
and shorter in winter.

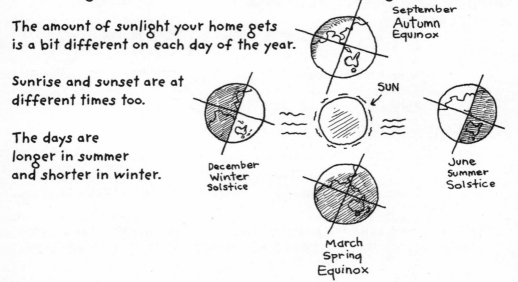

RISE AND SHINE

The Sun doesn't really RISE or SET. It just looks like that to us. We feel like we're standing still, but Earth is always spinning on its AXIS. That's the line between the two poles.

It gets dark at night because your part of the Earth isn't facing the Sun's heat and light.

If you lived at either of the poles you would have MONTHS of sunlight in summer and MONTHS of darkness in winter.

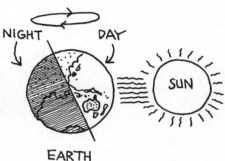

Earth's tilt and orbit changes a bit over tens of thousands of years.
That's why we get ICE AGES.
During the last ice age, about a quarter of Earth's land was ice.

The continents were in the same positions as they are today, but the sea level was much lower.
You could live and walk on land where there is now ocean.

That ice age ended about 12,000 years ago.
The sea level rose by about 120 m and giant animals like woolly mammoths and sabre-toothed cats became extinct.

When living things and non-living things
exist together in one environment that's an ECOSYSTEM.
A living thing's natural environment is its HABITAT.

Earth's natural environments aren't the same everywhere.
There are groups of similar ecosystems around the world.
They are called BIOMES.

There are TERRESTRIAL biomes on land and AQUATIC biomes in water.

Living things can change to suit their environment . . .

And some animals change
the environment to suit THEM.

Apartments

Offices

cities

Suburbs

Farm

Fishing

Port

The aim of the game is to live longer, eat better,
avoid being eaten and have more babies.

Humans have got VERY good at doing that.
There are about 7.8 billion people on Earth.
But we are hardly ever found in the wild these days.

Monkey
brothers
picnic

Our planet (mostly) looks after us.
Do you think WE are (mostly)
looking after our planet?

Paper, plastic, bubble wrap
cardboard, glass, styrene,

3

THE LIFE
BEFORE YOU

LIFE HAD TO START SOMEWHERE...

When life started on Earth
it was so different from us
it might as well have been an ALIEN.

We don't know how or exactly when or where on Earth
life first appeared, but it was probably in water.

It might have been created around
boiling volcanic vents in the ocean.

Life was just a single cell at first, and it was very VERY tiny.

But it was still AMAZING.

THREE
PRIMITIVE
SINGLE-CELL
MONKEY
LIFEFORMS

4.5 billion years ago, when Earth was a baby world, it was HOT. For a while the air was probably even made of vapourised rock. That's HOTTER THAN HOT. But as Earth started to cool and the oceans were formed, things got really interesting . . .

The earliest evidence of life is found in FOSSILS that are 3.5 billion years old.

We think of fossils as bones or shells or maybe wood that has turned into stone over millions of years.
Or we might think of preserved bits of a plant or animal, or an imprint in mud or clay that has hardened to rock.
But none of those things existed 3.5 billion years ago.

The earliest fossils are found in Australia.
They're rocks that once had bacteria in them, called STROMATOLITES.

Stromatolites don't look nearly as interesting as these guys.

Stromatolites can photosynthesise like a plant.
They are very rare these days,
but they used to be EVERYWHERE and they were VERY important . . .

FACT BOX

When we say LIFE we usually mean bacteria, plants and animals. A rock is not alive, but living things like stromatolites might make mounds that LOOK like rocks. Scientists don't all agree on what we mean when we say 'life', but usually if something can reproduce and grow and adapt and use energy it is considered alive. And that means it is made up of one or more cells. Living things are called ORGANISMS.

Over a LONG, LONG time, stromatolites made energy by photosynthesis.
They used up LOTS of carbon dioxide
and made LOTS of oxygen.

They made enough oxygen for other life to evolve.
But with less carbon dioxide in the air,
everything cooled down EVEN MORE.

It became too cool for the stromatolites,
and the air wasn't carbon-dioxidy enough.
Stromatolites were so successful that
they almost caused their own extinction.

CO2

I'm
d
sea
horse!

O2 →

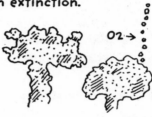

Stromatolites

By 800 million years ago, the percentage of oxygen
in the air was the same as it is now.

Plus, the ozone layer had formed.
And that protected Earth from the dangerous solar radiation.

So about 600 million years ago,
life REALLY kicked into gear.
And it was made of
more than one cell!

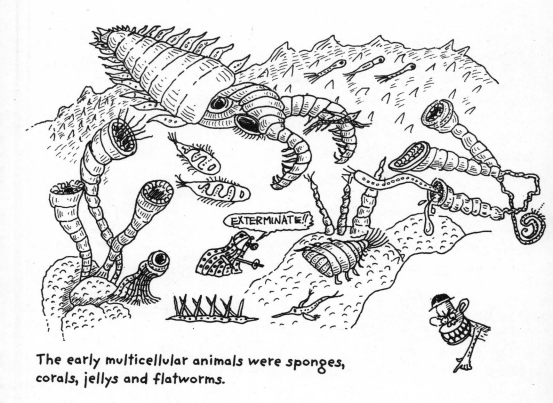

The early multicellular animals were sponges, corals, jellys and flatworms.

That's right, flatworms! Gross! And jelly! YUM!

Help!

very rare monkey-eating multicell.
(May be a fictional animal!)

Monkey eating
the monkey eating
the fact box.

I love jelly!

FACT BOX

ALL life on Earth has a common ancestor.
You. Me. Plants. Fungi! Bacteria! EVERY LIVING THING.
Scientists split life's ancient history into ERAS or
PERIODS. They help us to remember when the big
changes in the development of life happened. The first
period (the longest one) is called the PRECAMBRIAN.

Monkey eating
the fact box

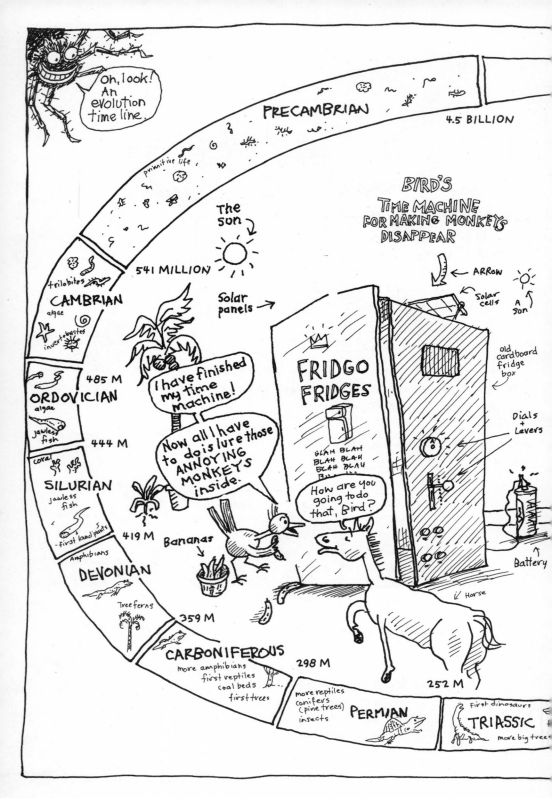

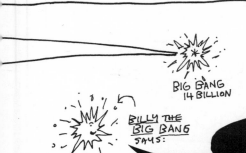

BIG BANG
14 BILLION

BILLY THE BIG BANG SAYS:

LOOK AT ALL THESE COOL THINGS I MADE!

PRECAMBRIAN Life appears in the oceans.
CAMBRIAN The main forms of life are algae and marine invertebrates. The land is dry and rocky.
ORDOVICIAN Fish arrive on the scene.
SILURIAN Coral grows, air-breathing animals appear and plants grow on the land.
DEVONIAN The age of fishes, ammonites and trilobites. Ferny forests cover the land. Amphibians leave the water to hang out in them.
CARBONIFEROUS Hello, reptiles, spiders and insects! Giant swamp forests grow on land.
PERMIAN The supercontinent Pangaea has been formed. Drought and freezing cold make life hard, but pine trees and reptiles change to suit.
TRIASSIC Dinosaurs! Mammals begin to appear.
JURASSIC Pangaea is breaking up, and life on land really takes off thanks to a warm, wet climate. Birds appear and animals are BIG!
CRETACEOUS Earth gets its first flowering plants.
TERTIARY Dinosaurs are extinct, but mammals, including the first primates, go wild.
QUATERNARY Early humans start to take over the world . . .

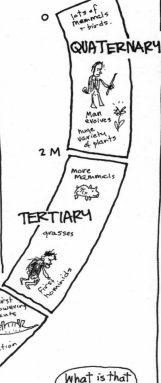

0
lots of mammals + birds.
QUATERNARY
Man evolves
huge variety of plants
2 M
more mammals
TERTIARY
grasses
first hominids
65 M
first flowering plants
Dinosaurs mass extinction
CRETACEOUS
145 M
Dinosaurs still rule!
201 M
Dinosaurs are King!
JURASSIC
Big forests   first birds

What is that bird up to?

73

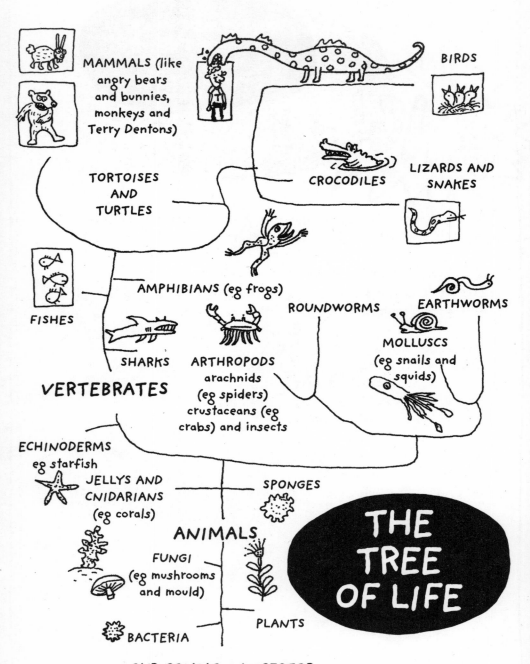

MAMMALS (like angry bears and bunnies, monkeys and Terry Dentons)

BIRDS

TORTOISES AND TURTLES

CROCODILES

LIZARDS AND SNAKES

AMPHIBIANS (eg frogs)

ROUNDWORMS

EARTHWORMS

FISHES

SHARKS

MOLLUSCS (eg snails and squids)

VERTEBRATES

ARTHROPODS arachnids (eg spiders) crustaceans (eg crabs) and insects

ECHINODERMS eg starfish

JELLYS AND CNIDARIANS (eg corals)

SPONGES

ANIMALS

FUNGI (eg mushrooms and mould)

BACTERIA

PLANTS

THE TREE OF LIFE

OUR COMMON ANCESTOR (basic life)

I don't like it much.

PROFESSOR TERRY DENTON IS RELATED TO MUSHROOMS

A very clever guy called Charles Darwin published his book ON THE ORIGIN OF SPECIES in 1859.

His research showed that life EVOLVED.
Evolution is like a tree with different types of living things very gradually 'branching' off from the trunk.

Lots of people didn't want to believe it.
And they got REALLY CRANKY when Darwin explained how humans were closely related to gorillas.
But we're not JUST related to gorillas.
ALL life is distantly related.

It's hard to believe that we all evolved from the same ancestor as a mushroom.

But it's true.

An excellent drawing of a gorilla →

I'm not happy about being related to humans either.

I don't like it much either

FACT BOX

Bacteria mostly only have one cell. Everything else has more than one. Mushrooms have millions.
The human body has TRILLIONS.

WHAT IS EVOLUTION?

Plants took AGES to evolve from algae into flowers.
But whenever the climate changed,
plants managed to evolve and survive.

FERNS went crazy in the Devonian period
when it was warm and humid.
They covered the land with forests.
Amphibians hopped out of the water to live there.
You can still find ferns in wetlands and the tropics.

GYMNOSPERMS are plants without flowers.
Fir trees evolved in the Permian period
when it was freezing cold.
They're very tough
and still grow in cold areas.

Finally we get to
ANGIOSPERMS
with their pretty
flowers.

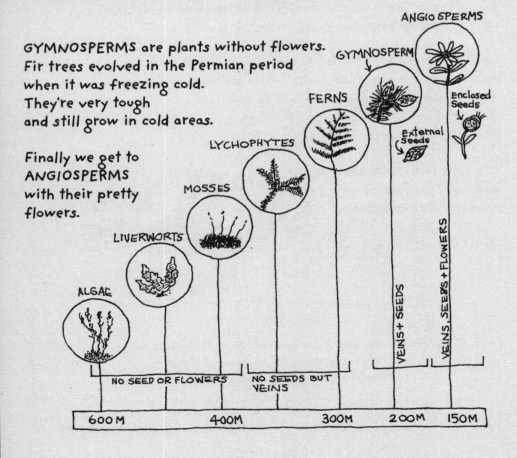

76

Nothing happens suddenly in evolution. Changes can take millions of years and millions of generations. Mostly changes only 'stick' if they are useful. In tiny steps, living things changed from those early single-celled organisms into the complex animals and plants we know today.

FUNGI branched off the tree of life
just before the animals did.
That was about 9 million years after plants.

Fungi can't make their own food.
They have to 'eat' and 'drink'.
Fungi are more like animals than plants.

SPORES are tiny cells that are released from the CAP, the bit of the mushroom we eat. They fly away on the wind.

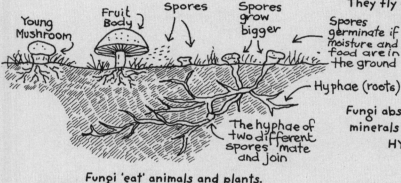

Young Mushroom

Fruit Body

Spores

Spores grow bigger

Spores germinate if moisture and food are in the ground

Hyphae (roots)

The hyphae of two different spores 'mate' and join

Fungi absorb water and minerals through their HYPHAE.

Fungi 'eat' animals and plants. Alive or dead! Mould living on old fruit is a fungus. And some fungi can even grow on our bodies. Gross!

A mushroom who's just a funguy

FAIRY RING

A circle of mushrooms that may grow to 10m in diameter.

FACT BOX

Yeast that makes bread rise is a fungus. And lots of medicines are developed from fungi. They can even clean up oil spills for us! Mushrooms are a type of fungi too. Most of them are deadly to humans, but others make a healthy snack.

EVOLUTION CHANGED ANIMALS AS WELL...

Dogs have been at our side for more than 15,000 years.
That's not long in evolutionary terms.

But now dogs come in an amazing variety of sizes and shapes,
from the tiny chihuahua to the weird but lovely bulldog
and the giant Saint Bernard.

SMALL

CURLY

BIG

STRAIGHT HAIR

SPOTTY

Of modern animals only dogs
have this great variety.

It's because people deliberately
picked out a certain dog with
certain characteristics.
Or a dog with an unusual colour or pattern.
Then they paired them with other dogs
with the same characteristics or look.

PLAIN

Wolves evolved about 1.5 million years ago
and ALL dogs are descended from one type of wolf. Now they are
a completely different species. But it wasn't just natural evolution that
made dogs so different, people had something to do with it.

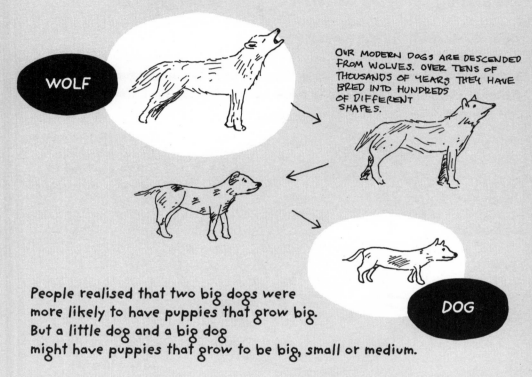

WOLF

OUR MODERN DOGS ARE DESCENDED
FROM WOLVES. OVER TENS OF
THOUSANDS OF YEARS THEY HAVE
BRED INTO HUNDREDS
OF DIFFERENT
SHAPES.

DOG

People realised that two big dogs were
more likely to have puppies that grow big.
But a little dog and a big dog
might have puppies that grow to be big, small or medium.

We needed dogs to suit all the different jobs we wanted them to do.
Hunting, herding or guarding, or following a scent or being ADORABLE.
All these jobs need different skills.
And different body shapes. And different noses and different fur . . .

FACT BOX

Your GENES decide what you look like. They can even decide
your behaviour, the illnesses you get and how long you live.
Everyone's genes are different, but animals of the same
species have similar genes. All dogs, for example, have more
genes linked to smell than humans. The more closely you are
related to someone, the more similar your genes will be.

To understand evolution, you have to understand about genes.
And to understand genes, you have to know about CELLS.
Remember the

HUGE

and possibly *INFINITE* Universe?

Now think small. REALLY small.
Not as small as an atom,
but smaller than a grain of sand. Smaller than the tardigrade.
Because even the tardigrade is made up of tiny cells all stuck together.

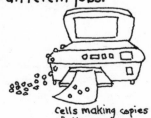

I am big for a tardigrade!

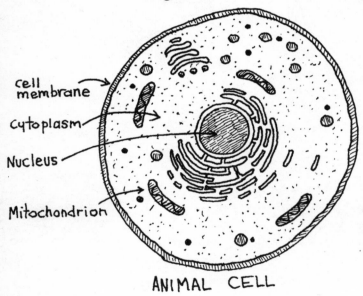

cell membrane

Cytoplasm

Nucleus

Mitochondrion

ANIMAL CELL

This is what an animal
cell looks like.
You can't see it
without a microscope.

The membrane is
like a teeny tiny
bag. Lots of very
useful bits are
floating inside.

Cells take in nutrients from food and turn them into energy.
And different types of cells in your body do different jobs.

Cells make copies of themselves
so you can grow and heal.

When they divide, the new cell is
USUALLY a perfect copy of the old one.

Cells making copies
of themselves.

Here is a plant cell.

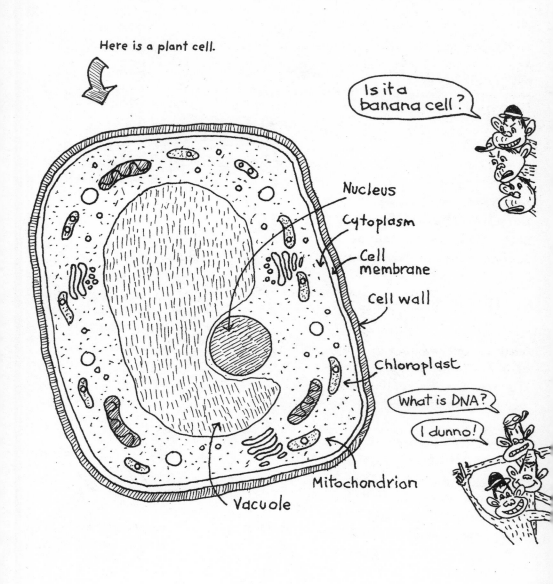

Is it a banana cell?

Nucleus

Cytoplasm

Cell membrane

Cell wall

Chloroplast

What is DNA?

I dunno!

Mitochondrion

Vacuole

Even though each copy of a cell SHOULD be the same,
each time a cell divides and copies there's a chance it might MUTATE.

A section of the DNA in the cell's NUCLEUS
might change, be inserted or deleted or moved around.
That's when evolution can occur.

We are all mutants!

DNA makes dogs different to cats.
It makes Butch different to Fifi and Spot.

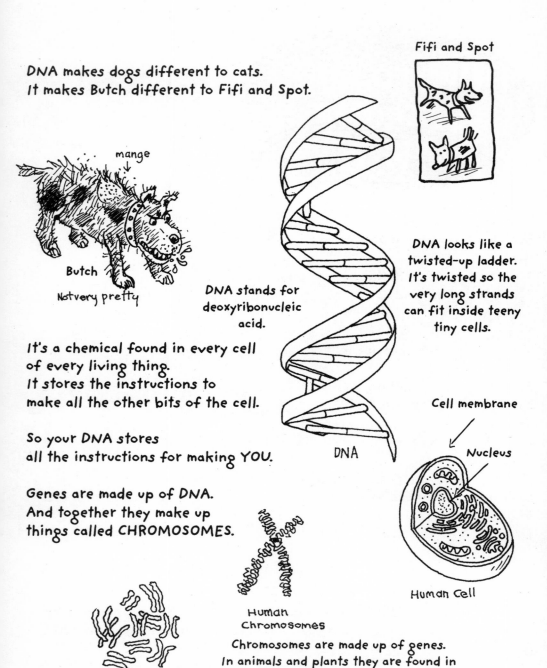

Fifi and Spot

mange

Butch

Not very pretty

DNA stands for
deoxyribonucleic
acid.

DNA looks like a
twisted-up ladder.
It's twisted so the
very long strands
can fit inside teeny
tiny cells.

It's a chemical found in every cell
of every living thing.
It stores the instructions to
make all the other bits of the cell.

So your DNA stores
all the instructions for making YOU.

Genes are made up of DNA.
And together they make up
things called CHROMOSOMES.

DNA

Cell membrane

Nucleus

Human Cell

Human
Chromosomes

Human genes

Chromosomes are made up of genes.
In animals and plants they are found in
the cell nucleus.

Any change in your DNA
is called a MUTATION.
But only some mutations can be inherited from your parents.

82

HOW TO MAKE A CLONE ARMY

You looking at me?

Even bacteria have chromosomes.

They reproduce by dividing their one cell.
Again and again and again . . .

The good news is the cells that make up
YOUR body clone themselves too.

Go, clone horse!!

The bad news is that doesn't mean you
can clone YOUR WHOLE BODY
like bacteria can
and take over the world with a clone army.

Most animals don't reproduce by dividing their whole bodies.
Humans, for example, usually have 23 pairs of chromosomes in each cell.
They're in pairs because we get a mix of genes
from our mum and dad.

Identical twins might have MATCHING DNA,
but they're NOT clones of their mum or dad.

Am I me,
or are you me?

And why do we only
have 3 legs?

Scientists HAVE cloned animals.
The first animal clone was a sheep.
She was called Dolly.

They are TRYING to clone extinct animals
like Tasmanian tigers and dinosaurs.
Because that would be COOL.

You can't fish Jurassic Park yet, but you've already met close relatives
of the dinosaurs. Birds! Yes, seagulls are

TINY FLYING T-REXES!

Some mammals can glide, but only bats can fly.
They still have five 'fingers' like other mammals
and can use each wing separately like arms.

But birds have more
in common with reptiles.
They lay eggs and
have scales on their feet.

Birds have EVEN MORE
in common with dinosaurs.
Lots of dinosaurs had
hollow bones and three toes
on each limb, like birds do.

They even had feathers.
Even though they couldn't fly.

Pterodactyls COULD fly.
But they were reptiles like crocodiles
and alligators. They weren't dinosaurs.
They evolved to fly on their own.

And went extinct without
passing flying on.

We are still waiting for
birds to invent
rocket-powered flight.

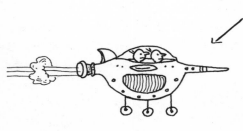

Animal flight didn't evolve all at once.
Bats, insects and birds all evolved to fly differently at different times.
If you can fly, you can escape predators and catch prey better than anyone else so it's a handy skill to have.

The Archaeopteryx was the first dinosaur that was like a bird.
But it had jaws and teeth and claws.
So you wouldn't dare get hot chips at the beach when they were around.

Hey, Bird. I'm flying!

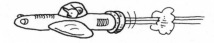

Evolution isn't an inventor.
When people were trying to breed a huge hunting dog, they were deliberately picking the biggest, strongest dogs . . .

But in nature there's NO PLAN.
The Archaeopteryx didn't DECIDE to evolve into a seagull.
It happened through NATURAL SELECTION.

Archaeopteryx

In the wild, mutations or behaviours that help you survive (or at least
don't get you killed) have a better chance of being passed down to your
kids. Then your kids might live to pass that mutation down to THEIR kids.
But when a trait stops being useful, your species is still stuck with it.

Some dinosaurs buried or covered their eggs.
Some reptiles, like crocodiles, still do.
But SOME dinosaurs made open nests on the ground
and sat on them.
Those dinosaurs evolved into modern birds.

When the climate got extreme,
keeping the temperature constant meant the chicks didn't die.
So those chicks got to grow up and lay eggs themselves . . .

Bad places for
a bird to nest.

Places that are
not bad, but
are not exactly
ideal, either.

Over millions of years, nests got more complex.

Birds don't need to be taught how to build them.
They JUST KNOW. That's called an INNATE BEHAVIOUR.

86

And if your species isn't a good fit for the environment
you either adapt, change your environment or become . . .

EXTINCT!

We are living on a changing planet.
And other animals and plants are evolving around us.
Something that used to be helpful can quickly STOP being useful.

Pugs are ADORABLE, and that's pretty useful when you're a pet.
But set a pug free and see how it goes hunting for its dinner . . .

That's SURVIVAL OF THE FITTEST.

A PREDATOR,
hunts and
eats PREY.

Confused prey.

This pug might
have to be a
SCAVENGER and
eat what predators
have left behind.

GRRR!
YAP! YAP! YAP!
YAP! YAP!

He's not
descended
from me.

Wolf

FACT BOX

There have been five MASS EXTINCTION EVENTS in
the history of life on Earth. That means that each time
between 75% and 90% of all the species alive disappeared
in one go. These events happened at the end of the
ordovician, devonian, permian, triassic and cretaceous
periods. After each mass extinction different types of life
evolved to fill the gap.

You've probably heard of the extinction of the dinosaurs about 65 million years ago.
It was pretty sudden.

A giant meteor might have hit the Earth or lots of volcanoes might have erupted.

Or both.

Prehistoric Bee ↓

Platypus ↓

Giant Prehistoric Cockroach ↙

Dead T-rex ↓

The word dinosaur means 'fearsome lizard'.
The word cockroach doesn't mean 'yuck'.
But it should.

Cockroaches, platypuses and bees survived the extinction of the dinosaurs.

As usual, changes to the climate caused the real trouble.
Only a quarter of life on Earth DIDN'T DIE.
Mostly small birds, reptiles, mammals, fish, insects and amphibians survived.

They rocked on into the Tertiary period and took over the world.

Did you know Spiders evolved 400M years ago. Dinosaurs 240M years ago. Dinosaurs died out 65M years ago. Spiders are still here!

ANOMALOCARIS were the scariest predators of the Cambrian ocean. They were like giant armoured prawns.

PLATYBELODONS were ancient elephants with giant mouths and two tusks shaped like shovels on their lower jaw.

Beware the mighty wombat! DIPRODOTON lived in Australia for AGES until it became extinct about 12,000 years ago.
It was a marsupial the size of a rhino.

Before people arrived in the Americas MEGAFAUNA roamed the land. Like huge SABRE-TOOTHED CATS that could take down a bison. And the truly enormous WOOLLY MAMMOTH.

A DODO.

The dodo was about a metre tall, had little useless wings, a bald head and some fancy little feathers on its bum. People discovered it in about 1598. They hunted it to extinction within 60 years.

The extinction of the dinosaurs wasn't the WORST extinction event.
THAT happened at the end of the Permian period.
It's called 'the Great Dying'.

Sharks survived, but about 96% of life became extinct.

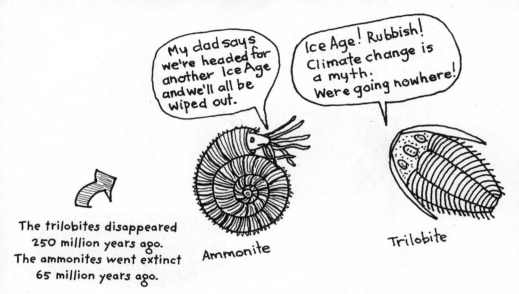

My dad says we're headed for another Ice Age and we'll all be wiped out.

Ice Age! Rubbish! Climate change is a myth. We're going nowhere!

The trilobites disappeared 250 million years ago.
The ammonites went extinct 65 million years ago.

Ammonite

Trilobite

Since people started to live in cities and burn fuels like coal and oil,
a record number of animals have become extinct.
Even more are under threat.
Now scientists are warning about a SIXTH mass extinction.
Guess who might be responsible for that one . . .

FACT BOX

Ancient platypuses probably lived alongside dinosaurs. These little mammals are very unusual. They lay eggs like a reptile, they feed their babies with milk that seeps through pores in their belly, they don't have teeth, but find food by sensing electric currents with their duck-like bills, and they have venom like spiders and snakes, but in spurs on their feet. They're one of the earliest branches of the mammal family tree.

DINOSAURS WERE AWESOME!

But if THEY were still around, WE probably wouldn't be. Mammals stepped up after dinosaurs became extinct, and we are a type of mammal called a PRIMATE.

THE PRIMATE FAMILY TREE

AUSTRALOPITHECUS (EXTINCT)

CHIMPANZEES AND BONOBOS

GORILLAS

ORANGUTANS

LESSER APES, LIKE GIBBONS

NEW WORLD MONKEYS, LIKE MARMOSETS AND HOWLER MONKEYS

OLD WORLD MONKEYS, LIKE BABOONS AND RHESUS MONKEYS

There are so many extinct branches of the primate family tree, and scientists are still finding evidence of new ones.
Our branch of the tree is called HOMO SAPIENS. Homo sapiens evolved at least 160,000 years ago, and lived alongside Neanderthals and Homo erectus for a while.

HOMO HABILIS
(EXTINCT)

HOMO ERECTUS
(EXTINCT)

US!
HOMO SAPIENS
(NOT EXTINCT!
HOORAY)

NEANDERTHALS
(EXTINCT)

You, chimpanzees, bonobos, gorillas and orangutans are all a special type of primate called a GREAT APE (or a HOMINID).

So our closest LIVING relatives on the primate family tree are
CHIMPANZEES and BONOBOS.
We share about 99% of their DNA.

Great apes have no tails, flat nails (not claws) and useful arms.
We have opposable thumbs.
Our thumbs touch our fingers so we can grip things.

Australopithecus had opposable toes as well as thumbs.

Australopithecus
could play PS4
with their toes.
Jealous?

Go, old girl!

AUSTRA

Homo sapiens DON'T have opposable toes,
because after Australopithecus we mostly walked on two legs.
Our feet started to look more like they do today.
We used them to walk ALL over the world.

Ha ha, I'm
walking on
your speech
balloon.

Hey, Bird, look
at me. I'm tight-
rope walking
upside-down on the
FACT BOX line

FACT BOX

Our common ancestor with chimpanzees lived about
7 million years ago. Chimps today can walk on two legs
if they want to and use wooden and stone tools. They
communicate using sounds, and can learn simple language.
They live in communities, they're omnivores, and their
babies have to be looked after until they're about five.
They understand trade, logic and enjoy doing puzzles.
They co-operate with each other and have emotions like
sadness and jealousy. Sound familiar?

Our bodies kept evolving until we became Homo sapiens.
Our teeth and jaw changed shape.
We got less hairy.
We developed better sweat glands,
and our vision became sharper
than our sense of smell . . .
Maybe because we hadn't invented deodorant yet.

Sniff!
Sniff!

Testing the sweat glands.

Eventually we evolved a bigger brain.
That might have been why we
developed complex language.

That's one of the things
that makes us DIFFERENT.

Other animals can
communicate with each other,
and sometimes with us.

I think therefore I am.

Well, Bird, the text says he does!

But do you really think?

UGH!

But Home sapiens have grammar. And writing.
And we have words that communicate
emotions and complex abstract ideas.

We communicated more and more
and worked together to plan
and become amazing inventors.

Eventually we replaced all the other human species.
But don't get too smug, big head!
Neanderthals had a bigger brain than we do.
And they STILL went extinct . . .

3½

THE LIFE
AROUND YOU

PETS AND DOMESTIC ANIMALS

One of the things that makes us different to other great apes is that we keep other animals in our homes and on farms. That's called DOMESTICATION.

MOST DRAGONS BEGIN LIFE AS AN EGG.

Wolves probably first hung around human camps for delicious leftovers.
The wolves that came in close but didn't attack became the ancestors of dogs.

Cats have been living with us since we grew crops.
Mice were stealing the stored food, and cats showed up to eat the yummy pests.

That worked for everyone except the mice.

Spiders eat pests that steal our food too.
But we don't like them as much as cats.

They evolved before the dinosaurs.
And they've been in our homes for as long as we've been building them.

Maybe THEY have domesticated US.

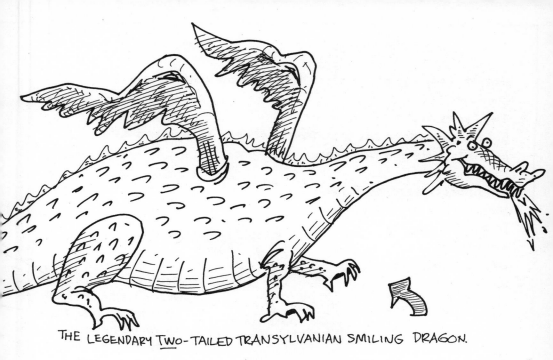

THE LEGENDARY TWO-TAILED TRANSYLVANIAN SMILING DRAGON.

Kept for its useful fire-starting skills, tough skin for leather and delicious eggs. Its two tails were useful to boil up and use as filling for meat pies. Did not make successful apartment pets.*

Goldfish weren't gold in the wild, and they started out as lunch.

In China, people started to keep the rare red, orange and yellow ones.

In the wild they were easy for predators to catch.
As pets they've been bred for a thousand years to look strange, decorative and colourful.

FACT BOX

*Dragons are fictional animals that exist in myths in many countries from England and Greece to Japan and China. They live in mountain caves, mostly sleeping and occasionally flying about breathing fire and setting people and cities alight. Would YOU keep one in an apartment?

Horses were one of the first things people painted and drew.
They were important as food.
But then people in the grasslands between Europe and Asia learnt to tame and ride them.

Wild horses were much smaller
than horses are today.
Most wild species
are extinct.
Only one species
survives in zoos.

Owl

Getting a wild horse to wear a saddle and train it to let you ride it is hard. Getting an owl to do the same is even more complicated.

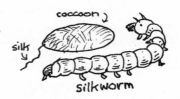

silkworm

There aren't many domesticated insects.
But Chinese silk worms have been making silk for us for 7,500 years.

Bees are domesticated too.
They were buzzing around before the dinosaurs,
so they must have been annoyed when
mammals started stealing their honey.

People first kept bees
9,000 years ago in North Africa.
They're not just important for their honey.
Bees pollinate our plants so we can
grow seeds, grain, fruit and vegetables.

Bee

As a form of transportation they didn't work out.

About 10,000 years ago people started to keep goats and sheep for meat, milk and their skin. Later they used their hair and fur to make wool.

In Southeast Asia, people kept chickens. But they didn't look like they do now. Now chickens are many times BIGGER than they were. They lay HUNDREDS of eggs a year instead of a couple.

YAY!

This doesn't seem right!!

Donkey

A male donkey is called a JACK and a female is called a JENNY! It's true!

AUROCHS were the ancestors of cows. You eat beef, wear leather and drink cows' milk because 10,000 years ago people tamed aurochs and bred them to be less scary.

Aurochs were taller than us, with massive curved horns. Their hobbies included goring hunters to death.

They used to be wild in Europe, Asia and Africa. There are now about 1.5 billion cows on Earth. But ZERO aurochs.

FACT BOX

Something is called an ANIMAL if it breathes oxygen, eats other plants or animals, can move and reproduce. The word SPECIES means 'a group that shares particular characteristics'. It's how we classify animals, fungi and plants. About 1.3 million animal species have been discovered (around 1 million of these are insects). Probably there are many more to discover. There might be up to 10 million!

THE FIRST VEGGIE PATCH . . .
At around the same time as people domesticated animals, they
had the idea to GROW plants rather than go out looking for them.

People couldn't resist making a few changes, though.
Bananas used to be a different shape and you couldn't peel them.
They looked like this before people first started to grow them.

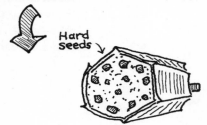

Hard
seeds

One banana is called a FINGER.
More than one is called
a HAND.

A whole bunch
is called a LUNCH.

More than one hand is
called a BUNCH.

The
monkeys
are
BACK!

Only about 300 years ago,
watermelons looked like this.

There was hardly any
delicious pink bit to eat.

Now it's ALL deliciousness.

We teleported
back through
this microwave.

DING!

Some plants were grown for food or materials to make things. Some because they looked pretty or were useful as medicines or drugs (like poppies for opium or barley for alcohol). Farming was one more reason to stay in one place and build towns and eventually cities.

Some plants can clone themselves.
They sprout from a piece of root, leaf or stem.
Or grow a runner, like grass does.

New banana plants grow from a RHIZOME,
an underground part of their stem.
Banana seeds aren't real seeds anymore.

Those Monkeys are back!

Noo!

Bad drawing of a telescope

In plants that have real seeds it works like this.

seeds germinate

Plant dies

Plant grows

Plant flowers

Plant makes fruit

Fruit releases seeds

People used to CROSS POLLINATE plants to make changes. They mixed pollen from one flower with pollen from another type of flower.

Now scientists can change the DNA of a plant to make it more resistant to disease or pests, grow more fruit, taste different or be healthier.
GENETICALLY MODIFIED plants are man-made mutants.

FACT BOX

Something is called a PLANT if it grows in one place and takes in water and nutrients through its roots. Plants use a chemical called CHLOROPHYLL in their leaves to photosynthesise, and their cell walls are made of something called CELLULOSE.

BACTERIA

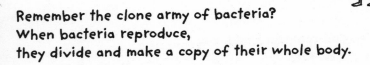

Remember the clone army of bacteria?
When bacteria reproduce,
they divide and make a copy of their whole body.

Because they're usually made of one cell,
they don't have to have babies, or pollinate flowers
or send out runners or spores.
That's why they can spread so quickly.

Bacteria are EVERYWHERE!
Some bacteria are harmful and can make you very sick.
But not all bacteria are disgusting.

Some bacteria that live in the sea
are BIOLUMINESCENT.

They make the water
and waves glow at night
with the most beautiful blues.

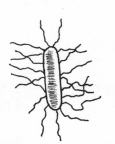

```
FACT BOX

There are so many different species of bacteria. Over 1,000
different types even live in your stomach. They're alive, but
they're not animals or fungi or plants. Some bacteria make
the same chemicals as animals' cells do, and some of them
can photosynthesise like plants. Stromatolites can clump
together to look like rocks, but bacteria don't join together
to make bodies and they don't have a nucleus in their cell.
They only have one or two circular chromosomes.
```

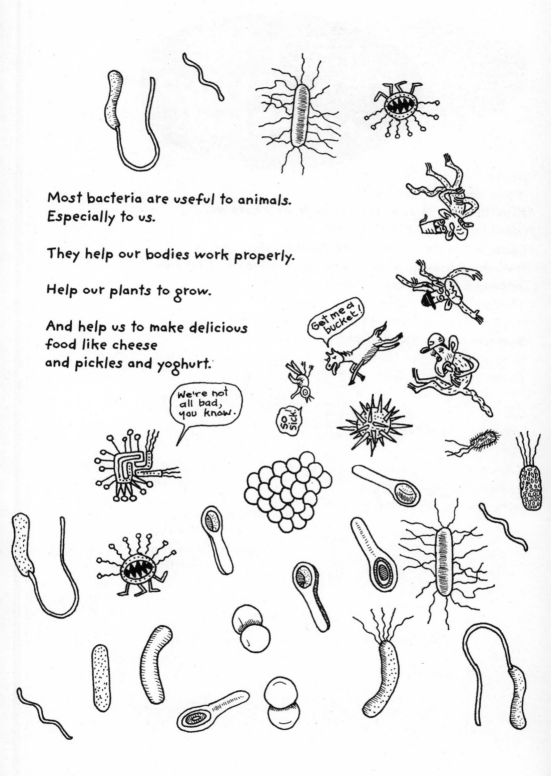

Most bacteria are useful to animals.
Especially to us.

They help our bodies work properly.

Help our plants to grow.

And help us to make delicious
food like cheese
and pickles and yoghurt.

MEET THE SPONGES AND CNIDARIANS

SPONGES live in the oceans and in fresh water.
A sponge's body is very simple.
It has lots of small holes, which filter the water.
That's how they feed on nutrients and take in oxygen.
They have ROOTS and can't move around.

Sponges haven't changed much since they first evolved.
They don't have blood, digestive systems or nerves.

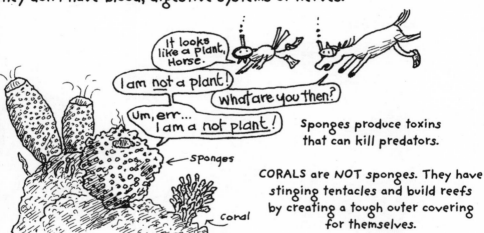

It looks like a plant, Horse.

I am _not_ a plant!

What are you then?

Um, err... I am a _not_ plant!

← Sponges

Coral

Sponges produce toxins that can kill predators.

CORALS are NOT sponges. They have stinging tentacles and build reefs by creating a tough outer covering for themselves.

FACT BOX

An *INVERTEBRATE* is an animal without a backbone.
They evolved earlier than the vertebrates so some of them
don't have sophisticated body organs and systems (like the
nervous system, circulatory system or digestive system).
Some invertebrates have an *EXOSKELETON*, a tough
covering on the outside of their body. Sponges, cnidarians,
molluscs, worms, echinoderms and arthropods
are all invertebrates.

Jellyfish and the colourful corals and sea anemones
are called CNIDARIANS.

JELLYFISH are soft invertebrates
that float around the ocean.

Some of them are see-through.

And some of them can create a
chemical reaction to glow in beautiful colours.

But WATCH OUT
they have a nasty stinger
at the end of their tentacles.

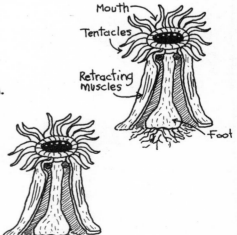

Mouth
Gut
Muscle ring
Tentacles

Oral arms
with stinging cells

Jellyfish stingers are called
NEMATOCYSTS.

Why the disguise?

He hates being called a Bumhead.

Under a jellyfish's bell-shaped
body is a kind of stomach.
Their mouth is there too,
which doubles as their bottom.

Mouth
Tentacles
Retracting muscles
Foot

SEA ANEMONES are beautiful.
They are called the flowers of the sea.
But they are DEFINITELY animals.

They catch and eat crabs and fish.
And some can be up to a metre wide.

MOLLUSCS, AHOY!

Squids have a shell *INSIDE* their body and defend themselves by squirting ink.

MOLLUSCS that live on land include snails and slugs. Clams, mussels, squids and octopuses are water molluscs.

Their soft bodies have a SHELL inside or out.

The simplest molluscs have one muscly FOOT. Land snails and slugs produce SLIME to protect their foot, stick to things and stop them drying out.

Eye Tentacles

SLUGS RULE

Feelers

SEA SLUG

All snails have a shell. It's a part of their body. They can't leave it.

In land snails the shell contains organs like their lungs.

Sea slugs don't need lungs so they breathe through gills around their BUTTS.

Snails have eyes on their top tentacles But no ears.

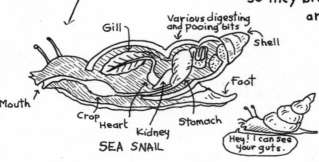

Gill

Various digesting and pooing bits

Shell

Foot

Mouth

Crop
Heart
Kidney
Stomach

SEA SNAIL

Hey! I can see your guts.

Octopuses are fierce hunters of the sea.
They live alone in DENS, which they decorate with things they find.
They attack creatures with shells by drilling a hole and injecting a
toxin or just pulling them apart and paralysing them with their saliva.

Their skin can change
colour and texture and
some can glow in the dark.

They can squirt black ink
and swim by
JET PROPULSION, by
shooting water behind them.

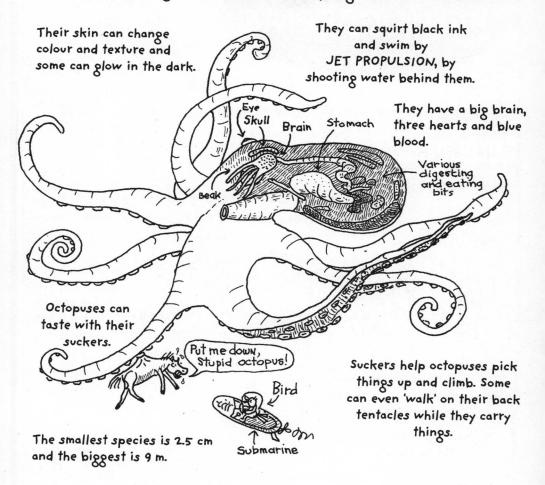

Eye
Skull
Brain
Stomach
Beak

They have a big brain,
three hearts and blue
blood.

Various
digesting
and eating
bits

Octopuses can
taste with their
suckers.

Put me down,
Stupid octopus!

Bird

Submarine

Suckers help octopuses pick
things up and climb. Some
can even 'walk' on their back
tentacles while they carry
things.

The smallest species is 2.5 cm
and the biggest is 9 m.

SHIP

Legends all around the world
tell of a giant octopus
as big as a ship.

Maybe they were real once,
or maybe they're still waiting to be discovered.

HELLO, WORMS AND ECHINODERMS

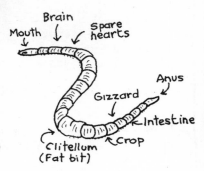

Inside a worm

Blood Vessel
Intestine
Muscles

Mouth
Brain
Spare hearts
Anus
Gizzard
Intestine
Crop
Clitellum (Fat bit)

WORMS might have a soft tube-shaped body.
And they might not have legs.
But they have a head, brain, blood and organs,
including five basic hearts.
Nice one, worms!

Most worms eat things found in water or soil,
but SOME worms live INSIDE other animals, even people.

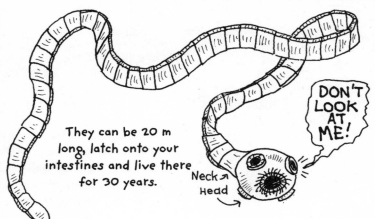

They can be 20 m long, latch onto your intestines and live there for 30 years.

Neck
Head

DON'T LOOK AT ME!

Tapeworms look like a long white ribbon. They can live in stomachs.

I'm a STAR!

ECHINODERMS are starfish and sea urchins.
Instead of blood, they pump water around
their bodies to get oxygen.
They have little suction-cup feet on tubes.
Starfish force their
prey's shell open with their feet,
then vomit their guts onto them.
It starts to digest the animal alive.

ALOHA, ARTHROPODS

You've met lots of ARTHROPODS in your life.

They live on land, in water and even in the air.
They have an exoskeleton.
And have a body with different segments
and a matching number of legs on each side.

That's right, it's just another name for BUGS!

Arachnids, insects and millipedes are all arthropods . . .
and CRUSTACEANS like lobsters and crabs
are the BUGS OF THE SEA.

To grow, arthropods have to shed their WHOLE exoskeleton.

Crabs MOSTLY walk sideways but some can walk forward or back.

The largest crabs are the Japanese spider crabs. Their leg span is 4 m.

Crabs 'speak' to each other by waving their claws.

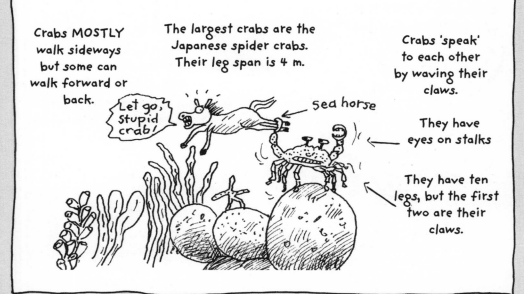

Let go, Stupid crab!

sea horse

They have eyes on stalks

They have ten legs, but the first two are their claws.

ARACHNIDS are spiders, mites, ticks and scorpions.
Their eight-legged bodies are divided into three sections.
They have a HEAD, THORAX and an ABDOMEN.
Most of them eat other animals, but their mouth isn't very big.
They have to break their food down before they eat it.

Spiders inject venom into their prey to paralyse or kill it.
Some spiders wrap it up in silk before or after that,
and inject digestive liquid into their prey's body.
That turns it into liquid.

Scorpions grab their prey
with their pincers
and chew it with their fangs.
But THEIR venom is at the end of their tail.

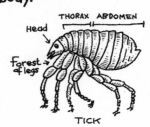

THORAX ABDOMEN
Head
Forest of legs

TICK

Ticks and some mites feed on blood.
A tick cuts into the skin
and inserts its feeding tube.
Yum! Is it lunch time yet?

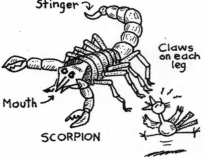

Stinger
Claws on each leg
Mouth
SCORPION

Yikes!

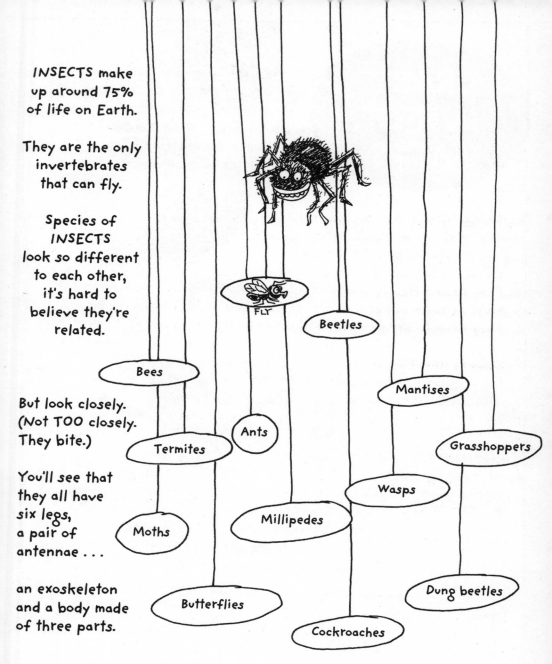

INSECTS make up around 75% of life on Earth.

They are the only invertebrates that can fly.

Species of INSECTS look so different to each other, it's hard to believe they're related.

But look closely. (Not TOO closely. They bite.)

You'll see that they all have six legs, a pair of antennae ...

an exoskeleton and a body made of three parts.

FLY

Beetles

Bees

Mantises

Ants

Grasshoppers

Termites

Wasps

Moths

Millipedes

Butterflies

Dung beetles

Cockroaches

I HATE SPIDERS!

Me, too.

FLY

We call insects PESTS, but if they disappeared the soil wouldn't be healthy, plants wouldn't be pollinated, dead things wouldn't decompose properly and other animals wouldn't have anything to eat.

113

CRAZY INSECT FACTS

WASPS can be so small that you can barely see them. Or they can be as big as your hand. Most adult wasps eat nectar from flowers. But their LARVAE ONLY eats animals.

Wasps

Australian spider wasps sting their prey to paralyse it. They drag the poor spider to the nest and lay an egg on it.

When the baby wasp hatches, it starts eating right away. And the spider gets EATEN ALIVE.

A flying horse

She eats stuff alive too. Serves her right

Poor Spider

Eaten alive by a BABY WASP! Are you kidding me?

GRRR!!

Grasshoppers

A GRASSHOPPER can eat 16 times its own weight in plants.

BEETLES

BEETLES are different to other flying insects. Two of their four wings are hard covers that protect their delicate flying wings.

Moths

FACT BOX

Insects and cnidarians and amphibians don't look the same at different stages of their life. Most insects lay eggs, which hatch into larvae. A caterpillar is the LARVAL PHASE of a moth or butterfly's life. A maggot is the larval phase of a fly's life. Once a larva has eaten enough, it moults its skin a few times, spins a little silk sleeping bag called a COCOON or turns into a shiny hard PUPA.
Inside it is transforming into its adult self.

A MILLIPEDE is a long, segmented insecty thing.
Some are just under 40 cm long.
Just because 'milli' means a thousand,
doesn't mean they have 1,000 legs.
Some have 30 legs and some have 400 legs.

A rhinoceros is not an insect and is hard to spell. They have four legs and a large horn on their face. In medical dictionaries 'rhino' means 'nose'. So THEIR name make sense. Unfortunately there is no such thing as a milloceros.

Millipedes

Ants are found everywhere except the Arctic and Antarctica.
But you've probably only seen the WORKER ANTS.
They're all female and they don't have wings.
Male ants have wings, like queen ants,
but THEY only live for about a week.

Ants

Ants might be little, but they are tough.
They can carry 50 times their body weight.
And work together to carry even bigger things.

Termite

Oi, Antface! That's our house!! Put it back!

Crazy Ant

Termite

Termites eat wood, including our houses. They are NOT ants. They're more closely related to cockroaches. Some of them build giant mounds up to 30 m wide.

cockroaches

EVEN CRAZIER INSECT FACTS

A CICADA
Actually it's a drawing of a Cicada.

Male cicadas sing by vibrating a part of their body. Cicada larva hatch above ground and dig down to suck on tree roots. Then they all come to the surface at the same time to turn into adults and make a LOT of noise.

AUGH!

Mantis

Praying mantises are ninjas of camouflage and hunting.
They look like sticks and leaves, have strong chomping jaws, sharp front legs and can jump like cats.
They even catch and eat small birds.
Some look just like flowers.
Insects that come to collect pollen stay to become lunch.

YUM!

DO YOU MIND!

Butterflies

All animals need a BIT of salt to survive.
But they can't buy a pack of crisps.
Some butterflies flutter down to drink the tears of turtles.
Some even drink crocodile tears. It's called LACRYPHAGY.

Flies lay eggs that hatch into maggots.
Maggots eat dead things like
uncovered food, rubbish,
dead bodies, even rotting flesh.

They don't have legs,
but they DO have mouths
with hooks on them.

FLY

Flies taste with their feet.
They vomit digestive juices onto your food,
then suck it up with their straw mouths.

FUN FACT: Both flies and maggots are

DISGUSTING!!!

But are they MORE disgusting than
cockroaches? You be the judge.

Cockroaches haven't changed in 200 million years.
You can't improve on perfection.
They can eat ANYTHING, but can go a month without food.
They can have 20,000 babies a year,
hold their breath for seven minutes, survive dangerous radiation
and live almost a week without their head.
Their hobby is carrying bacteria from the bin to your benchtop.

POLLINATION AND HONEY

Beehives have a queen bee,
female worker bees and male drones.
Only the queen and the workers have stings.
The queen uses hers to lay eggs.

sting

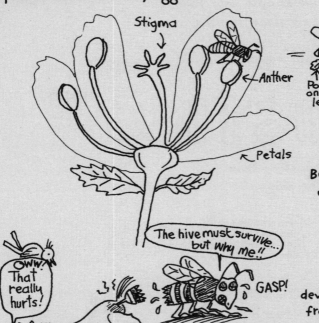

Stigma

Anther

Pollen on back legs

Petals

The hive must survive... but why me!!

OWW! That really hurts!

GASP!

But when a worker bee uses its sting, it DIES.

For fruit or seeds to develop, pollen needs to go from the ANTHER of one plant to the STIGMA of another.

FACT BOX

A special relationship between two organisms is called SYMBIOSIS. When both of the organisms benefit, it's called MUTUALISM. When one benefits, it's called COMMENSALISM. You already know the third type, PARASITISM. Ticks and tapeworms both do that. If there is a parasite and a host, then one of the organisms in the relationship suffers.

Bees and plants have a special relationship. Flowers have a smell when they are ready for pollination. Bees follow their sweet scent to the flower because THEY need to collect pollen and take it back to the hive. As bees go flower to flower, they drop some pollen. They spread it around, and that's how the plant reproduces.

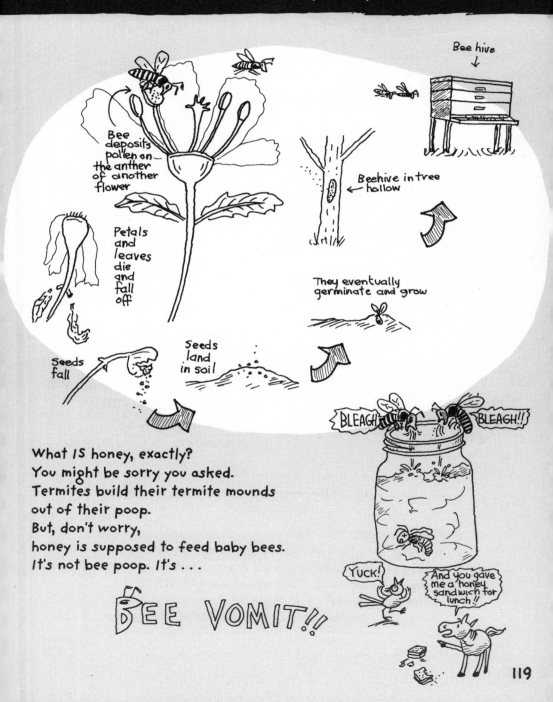

Bee hive ↓

Bee deposits pollen on the anther of another flower

Beehive in tree ← hollow

Petals and leaves die and fall off

They eventually germinate and grow

Seeds land in soil

Seeds fall

What IS honey, exactly?
You might be sorry you asked.
Termites build their termite mounds
out of their poop.
But, don't worry,
honey is supposed to feed baby bees.
It's not bee poop. It's . . .

BEE VOMIT!!

BLEAGH! BLEAGH!!

YUCK!

And you gave me a honey sandwich for lunch!!

119

THE FOOD CHAIN

When one plant or animal eats another, that's called a FOOD CHAIN. But because animals don't just eat one food, it's really more like a complex FOOD WEB.

Spiders and cats are CARNIVORES.

Carnivores can only eat meat. They can't digest plants.

Rhinos are HERBIVORES. They only eat plants.

A rhino will happily KILL YOU. But it won't EAT YOU. It will leave you for scavengers like the hyenas.

FACT BOX

Plants can make their own energy. They mostly don't need anything more than photosynthesis to get the energy they need, and some bacteria can use energy from chemicals in their environment. These are called AUTOTROPHS. They are the base of all the food chains in the world. Everything else is called a HETEROTROPH. The eaters!

It's a dog. ↓

Dogs eat whatever they can get their hungry little paws on. They are OMNIVORES, like people (mostly). Omnivores can eat both plants and animals.

At the top of every food chain is an APEX PREDATOR. The apex predator has no natural predators.

Humans domesticated apex predators, like the wolf and birds of prey to help them hunt.

How come we aren't apex predators?

Bananas think we are!

Cormorants are mostly wild. But in Japan and China, they are trained to catch fish for their owners. →

Hey, Bird could I eat that baby for lunch?

No, Horse! For 2 reasons: You're a herbivore, and you're only a drawing of a horse.

Tools and smarts have made YOU a kind of apex predator, even though there are lots of animals that could easily have you for lunch.

But there's one group that eats even the most fearsome apex predator. The DECOMPOSERS.

I'm a hero!

They break down waste and dead material and keep the whole food chain going. Fungi and bacteria, and animals like earthworms, cockroaches and maggots might be revolting, but they're food-chain heroes!

WHOSE POO IS THAT?

"It says: "Poo!""

HA. HA. HA.

There's nothing funny about poo, boys.

What's for lunch, Bird?

Poo. Do you want some?

Suddenly, I'm not hungry.

Okay, let's get SERIOUS about poo.

SOME ANIMALS EAT POO!

Their own or others'.

Some insects eat the poo of large animals because there's still lots of undigested food in there. Dung beetles have been rolling animal poo around for about 30 million years. They eat it, and they lay their eggs in it.

Dung beetles

Rabbits do two DIFFERENT TYPES of poo. Only one is for eating, though.

Some baby animals even eat their mama's poo to get useful bacteria that they don't have at birth.

Mum! This is the worst chocolate I've ever had!

tree

Wombats are a BIT cube-shaped.
Their butts are not.
But their poos are the only
cube-shaped poos in the world.
No one really knows how or why.

You can identify the animal that pooped
by looking at its poo.
And you can tell what it ate for dinner.

Well, I'm normal,
I just poop out
poo.

Snakes don't poop much,
but when they do they poop
out solid wee as well.

snail poo

snail head

Because snail's bodies are all twisted up in their shell,
snail butts are in their lungs and just near their head.

When bears sleep for the winter
they don't poop the WHOLE TIME.
How? Do you REALLY want to know?

Furry plug

They lick their fur,
and their body makes
a kind of furry plug.

That means they CAN'T poop until they eat again in spring.

Lots of animals poop to mark their territory.

Big cats like lions and tigers want other
predators to know they're there.

But small cats aren't apex predators,
so they bury theirs to hide their smell.

Whatcha doing
down there, H?

I'm burying my poo
because I'm not
an apex predator.

POPPING
OFF

Almost all mammals fart.
Sloths seem to be the only mammals that don't.
But they have SERIOUSLY bad breath.

Whales do the biggest.
Seals do the stinkiest.

For some fish it's life or death.
If they don't fart, they'll float to the surface and die.

Sea cows use their gas to float.
When they need to sink again, they just let one rip.

There are so many teensy weeny termite farts every day that together they contribute to the world's methane pollution.

Even roaches fly by fart power.

*

*Don't you wish this was true?

Some snakes have a
farty defence mechanism
called CLOACAL
POPPING.

FACT BOX

When mammals break down food in their gut, gas is
produced. That's thanks to a certain type of bacteria needed
to digest our food. Plant diets produce MORE gas, but meat
diets are STINKIER. The longer an animal's digestive
system is, the more chance for gas to be produced.
Octopuses, mussels and clams DON'T fart.
Birds MIGHT. But no one really knows for sure.

ANIMALS ARE EVERYWHERE

Remember the tardigrades?
They're related to arthropods.

If things get too dangerous,
they go into a type
of hibernation.
It's called a TUN STATE.
They get rid of the water in their body
and turn into a lifeless ball for a while.
They can survive in dangerous radiation
and the cold vacuum of space.

Tardigrade asleep ↓

Z

Tardigrade in tun state

Z!

Actual Size

Tiny Hot water bottle

stick

Also called moss piglets or water bears.

Tardigrades, tubeworms, clams and shrimp can live
near the boiling water of undersea volcanic vents.

Animals living in sunless caves
are white and have no eyes.
You don't need colour or sight in the dark.

There are animals living in
the deepest darkest places in the ocean
where the temperature is nearly freezing.

And some animals even live ON and INSIDE other animals.

Beavers chop down trees with their teeth to build dams and homes of mud and branches. Termites dig tunnels with huge mounds on top. They even build tall chimneys to let any hot air out. Some animal homes are weird and wonderful.

SWIM WITH FABULOUS FISHES

SHARKS and FISH were the first vertebrates.
They live and breathe underwater with their gills.

Not ALL fish have scales. Some are covered in SLIME.

Sharks and rays are fish, but there's a big difference.
Their skeleton is made of something called CARTILAGE.
And fish are bony.

Rays have flat bodies
and a stinger on their tail.

Slow down, you guys!

But it's sharks who are the
apex predators of the ocean.

They are very clever,
with strong jaws
and rows of teeth for tearing you to pieces.

Some sharks don't lay eggs.
They give birth to live babies.
Sand tiger sharks are even predators before they are born.
They eat their siblings until they're the only one left.

FACT BOX

A VERTEBRATE has a BACKBONE of cartilage or bone
protecting the spinal cord. Cartilage isn't as hard as bone.
It's a bit flexible and usually joins bone together. Feel your
ear. It's made of cartilage. BONE has a tough outside layer
and a spongy inside with blood vessels, nerves and bone
marrow. Fish, amphibians, reptiles, birds and mammals
are all vertebrates.

Most fish, even eels,
are RAY-FINNED fish.
Their fins are skin
stretched over bone.

Electric eels create a powerful
electric current in their bodies.
They use it to detect prey
and then stun it.

Some catfish have BARBELS,
whiskers near their mouth
that have tastebuds in them.
But some can taste with
their WHOLE BODY.

Me eat bird

Eeek! Go away, ugly catfish!

Seahorses don't look like fish.
But they are.

They're not great swimmers
so they hang onto things
with their tail.

Do you mind if I hang out here with you guys?

AMAZING AMPHIBIANS

Frogs eggs →

Grow into embryos →

fried frog's egg
Not so tasty

In Greek the word AMPHIBIAN means 'to lead a double life'. And that's exactly what toads, frogs, salamanders and newts do.

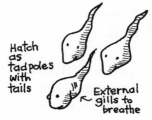
Hatch as tadpoles with tails
← External gills to breathe

We all look different when we're babies. But when amphibians are young, they have gills and look just like fish.

Tadpoles grow hind legs

When they grow up, they have four legs and lungs.

They survive on the food in their tails
Tadpoles grow front legs →

Tail gets shorter

Amphibians don't usually make cocoons or pupa, like insects, but their METAMORPHOSIS is just as amazing.

Adult frog

Amphibians breathe air as adults. But their skin always needs to be wet. They can't go too far from their watery home.

So cold!

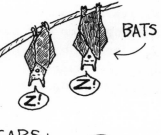

BEAR THAT THINKS SHE'S A BAT

Z!

Fish, amphibians and reptiles are COLD-BLOODED.
When the weather is frosty, they get frosty too.
Their body slows right down.
But some frogs don't just sleep through the winter.
They freeze,
and stop breathing completely.

Their heart stops beating.

They SEEM dead, but they're
ready to wake up again in spring.

BATS

Z! Z!

BEARS

Z! Z!

FACT BOX

Some mammals sleep when it's cold, too, even though
they're warm-blooded. Bats HIBERNATE hanging upside
down and all their body functions slow right down.
Bears don't hibernate in the same way, but they do go into
a very deep sleep for a long time. They have to be lovely
and fat before winter comes to survive. Some birds can
slow their heart and breathing down to survive short
cold periods, as well.

RENOWNED REPTILES

Snakes, crocodiles, alligators,
lizards and turtles all have
lungs and breathe air.
They are vertebrates with
scales, which they sometimes
shed with their skin
all in one go.

The biggest REPTILE is the six-metre-long saltwater crocodile.
They ambush their prey from the water.
And can kill large animals with a DEATH ROLL.

The smallest, cutest reptile is a chameleon.
They only have two 'fingers' on each hand.
And they can change their skin colour.
They have a handy tail for grasping
and a sticky tongue for catching dinner.

Damn you,
sticky tongue!

Poor Turtle.

Bum breathing

GASP!

Some things reptiles can do
are definitely strange.

Water turtles spend winter
in ice-covered ponds,
but they still need to breathe
and they can't freeze like a frog.
Luckily special blood vessels in their butt take oxygen from the water.
And, yes, it's known as BUM BREATHING.

FACT BOX

Cold-blooded animals rely on the environment to heat up
and cool down. They have to lie in the sunlight to
warm up. Or cool down in cool water. WARM-BLOODED
animals use energy in their bodies to warm themselves.
Plus they can SHIVER, twitching their muscles to warm up.
And PANT so they don't overheat. Mammals can sweat too,
which cools them down.

EGG FACTS

Reptile babies start out in eggs.
Reptile eggs are soft
and the shell is leathery.
Usually they are buried.
Mostly Mum doesn't wait around.
Although croc mums do.
So DON'T MESS WITH CROC EGGS.

The eggshells of reptiles,
birds and mammals are waterproof.
And inside is a sack
of fluid that protects the EMBRYO.

Amphibian eggs don't have any fluid
so they have to lay them in water.

It's quite unusual to have live babies.
Most types of animals lay eggs.

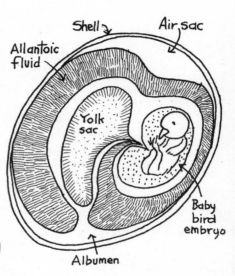

Shell
Air sac
Allantoic fluid
Yolk sac
Baby bird embryo
Albumen

Oops!

Fish lay TONS of tiny eggs.
A few carry them around in
their mouth until they hatch.
Seahorse dads carry them
in a belly pouch.

Some spider mums carry their
eggs around on their back.
And a few insects, like earwigs,
stay to look after their eggs too.

DANGEROUS ANIMALS

Humans are only at the top of the food chain because we work together, domesticate other animals and use tools. But lots of other animals are born with built-in weaponry.

Never trust a guinea pig.

BIG HEAVY THING →

ANGRY GUINEA PIG
(who can throw BIG HEAVY things a long way)

Goldfish do not appreciate reality tv.

Family   TV

And it's not always sharp teeth and claws.

Hippos are round and cute, but they are also HUGE and seriously aggressive.

TV-hating goldfish.

Even though they're herbivores, they're the world's deadliest large land animal. They can bite a crocodile in half.

The white rhino is just as huge and even heavier (and confusingly is grey). Its skin is like armour, and its massive horn is terrifying.

ANGRY ANT looking for revenge.

In a fair fight, a rhino MIGHT beat a hippo. But hippos live in groups, and they lurk around underwater. You won't even see them there, but disturb them and DIE!

A GIANT SPIDER TAKE-OVER!

SPIDER LANGUAGE FOR...

Spiders like to think THEY are the most dangerous creatures out there. But even some birds are poisonous if you attack or eat them. Not cranes. They're the tallest flying birds, but are harmless.

Birds called hooded pitohuis absorb and store toxins from the venomous insects they have for dinner.

Some fish and sea turtles can make themselves poisonous too.
They eat toxic algae, coral and jellyfish.

Cane toads make their own
incredibly dangerous poison
in their bodies.

Giant
Deadly
Tarantulas

Very
deadly

Hooded
Pitohui

ANIMALS YOU SHOULD NOT EAT!

Certain
Monkeys

Poison Dart Frog

Dung Beetle

Bats

Cane Toad

Some Sea Turtles

The poison dart frog's black-and-yellow
patterned skin is very pretty,
but it's actually a warning sign.

The box jellyfish is the gold medal winner
for most venomous animal.

Their toxin will DEFINITELY kill you.
But it's SO PAINFUL
that you'll probably have
heart failure first or go into shock and drown.

AND DEADLIEST OF ALL...

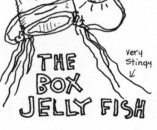

1

very
Stingy

THE
BOX
JELLY FISH

Me! Deadly!

The sweet
slow and
very deadly
slow
loris

← Tree

Venomous mammals are rare.
But there are a few.
This fuzzy little cutie is the slow loris.
It's ADORABLE.
But both its sweat and saliva
are venomous. And when the slow loris
combines them . . .
things get even more nasty.

PREDATOR PLANTS

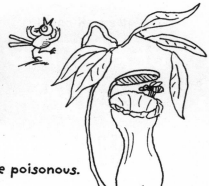

Pitcher plants

Everyone knows that some plants are poisonous.
But plants can be predators too.
They still photosythesise to get energy,
but they also get nutrients from their prey.
Different carnivourous plants evolved
in areas where the soil was too thin or not fertile enough.

Looks harmless.

The pitcher plant usually traps insects,
but it can even trap rats.

And the Venus flytrap doesn't
just eat flies. Some have been found
with frog skeletons inside.

I think monkeys are dangerous animals, Bird.

The next page will spell DOOM for the monkeys.

Venus fly trap.

FACT BOX

POISONOUS means something is dangerous if touched
or swallowed. VENOMOUS means the creature can sting
or bite. The Asian tiger snake and the blue-ringed octopus
are overachievers. They are both poisonous and venomous.

BEAUTIFUL BIRDS

BIRDS are warm-blooded vertebrates with beaks and feathers. They lay hard-shelled eggs. Their feathers keep them warm and help them fly. But they have wings even when they CAN'T fly.

Some birds, like penguins, 'fly' underwater. Their waterproof feathers keep them warm and dry.

Flamingos are a fabulous pink. That's because they eat algae and little shellfish that have an orange chemical called beta carotene in them.

I'm a flamingo. I can wade without getting my bum wet.

I can't.

I can sing, Horse!

I have wings, Bird.

Birds have a unique voice box that other animals don't have. Some birds can copy ANY sound, even the sounds of other animals. And every songbird has a different song.

FACT BOX

Lots of birds avoid the winter by flying to warmer places. That's called MIGRATION. The Arctic tern has the distance record. It flies for most of the year, travelling between the north pole and the south pole. Some butterflies and the Arctic caribou also migrate to avoid the winter. Caribou are reindeer so they DON'T fly. Except to deliver presents on Christmas Eve obviously.

I am the Best!!

Lots of birds just eat seeds and fruit.
But most birds are omnivores.
Some even eat other birds.

Parrot

Drumstick

Drumstick

Banana

Birds have TINY brains.
But they have LOTS of nerve cells
packed in there.
They are SMART.

The African grey parrot is
so smart it can learn and
understand hundreds of words.

It's not hard to see that birds
evolved from dinosaurs.
Owls swallow their prey whole.
Then they vomit up pellets made
of bones and fur.

Birds of prey have curved beaks
and sharp talons to tear at flesh.

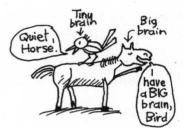

The secretary bird STOMPS its prey to death.
And guess what the monkey-eating eagle has for tea?

MARVELLOUS MAMMALS

Mammals are warm-blooded.
And the mums feed their babies on milk they make in their body.
Mammals breathe air and are hairy
(even whales have hair before they're born).

Some swim, some glide, some run and jump, but only bats can fly.
Mammals have teeth that are sharp or blunt depending on what they eat.
Whales don't have any at all.

Mammals all started out with four limbs.
The whales and dolphins didn't need them, so they evolved without them.
Mammals have claws, nails or hooves at the end of their limbs.

You already know
lots about mammals.
Because YOU ARE A MAMMAL.

But never forget.
Monkeys are
the BEST mammal!

ALL mammals have lungs.

Even dolphins have to swim
to the surface to breathe
through the BLOWHOLE on
the top of their head.

Some mammals have HORNS.
But horns are not all the same.

Rhino horns are made of KERATIN.
That's what nails are made of.
The horn grows all through their life.

Male deer have ANTLERS made of dead bone.
They shed them every year.
And giraffes just grow little bony bumps under their skin.

Elephant TUSKS are LIKE horns.
But they're actually giant teeth.
A narwhal tusk is long and pointy.
Narwhals are called the unicorns of the sea.

Excuse me but I am an omnivore.

Help!

Each mammal species has a unique set of SOUNDS.
Snorting, purring, barking and neighing . . .
Except giraffes who are silent.
Narwhals and dolphins whistle and click.

Monkeys sound the most like us.
They chat in what sounds like sentences.
Chimps, who are more like us in other ways,
use gestures more than sounds.

Howler monkeys are the
loudest land animal.

Quiet!

HOWL!

HOWL!

Quiet!

Quiet!

FACT BOX

Mammals come in all shapes and sizes, from the giant blue whale to the tiny bumblebee bat. But there are only three main types of mammals. MARSUPIALS have their young in pouches, MONOTREMES lay eggs and PLACENTAL MAMMALS have their young inside their bodies in a womb. Mammals like horses can find food and walk as soon as they are born, while human babies are helpless. But all mammals stay to care for their babies.

4

THE UNIVERSE IN YOU

WHAT IS IN YOU?

92% of your body is made up of carbon, oxygen, hydrogen and nitrogen. 60% of it is H_2O – water.

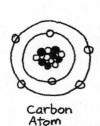

Carbon Atom

Carbon is the main ingredient in your muscles, fat, proteins and DNA. You're made of the same thing diamonds are made of.

Your body is made of many bits. *

- [ ] A brain box
- [ ] A brain
- [ ] A mind
- [ ] A monkey
- [ ] A pumpy thing (heart)
- [ ] A breathy thing (lungs)
- [ ] A liver
- [ ] A steering wheel
- [ ] Two kidneys
- [ ] An engine
- [ ] Ten fingers (including thumbs)
- [ ] Ten toes
- [ ] One tongue

- [ ] Two pieces of pie
- [ ] A horse
- [ ] A long intestine with lots of lumpy things attached
- [ ] A bum
- [ ] A spare bum
- [ ] Some private parts
- [ ] Two legs
- [ ] Two arms
- [ ] Another seven legs
- [ ] A big piece of cheese
- [ ] Leg bones
- [ ] Eyes (two)
- [ ] Lips (two)

* Some items on this list are not strictly accurate.

144

You are a vertebrate.
Only 2% of animals are vertebrates so you are RARE.

Vertebrates evolved an awesome brain, nervous system and skeleton.
And yours is one of the awesomest in the animal kingdom.

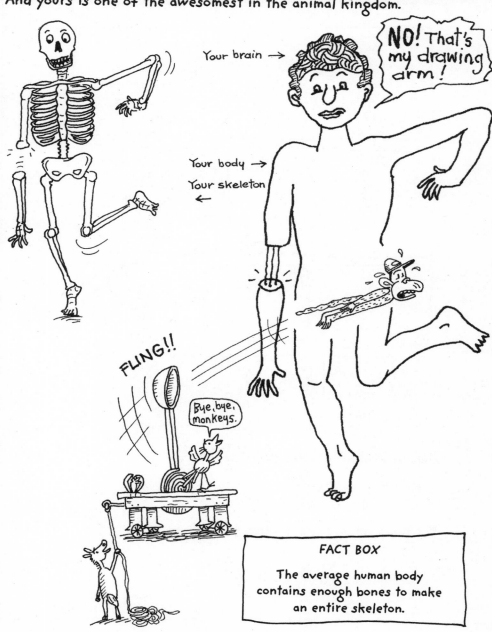

Your brain →

NO! That's my drawing arm!

Your body →

Your skeleton ←

FLING!!

Bye, bye, monkeys.

FACT BOX

The average human body contains enough bones to make an entire skeleton.

The Universe OUTSIDE you is BIG.

VERY BIG.

But the part of the Universe that IS you is

JUST AS BIG!

To the tiny things that make up your body, you are . . .

HUGE.

Even though the part of the Universe that IS you is

INFINITELY small!

The smallest bits in your body that you can know and name are just the ones we can see with our best microscopes.

Shrunk to the size of a bean, Bird and Horse set off to explore the wonders of the human body.

And even the simplest life has amazing worlds inside them.

You are a WHOLE UNIVERSE of cells
made up of molecules,
made up of about
7,000,000,000,000,000,000,000,000,000 atoms,
made up of WAY MORE sub-atomic particles.

And don't forget that every atom in your body is billions of years old.
Your hydrogen atoms were created in the BIG BANG.

SPARE PARTS

Your body would still work if you lost an arm or a leg.
But not if you were missing your heart or your lungs.

If you need a spare of those,
someone has to give you THEIRS.

Doctors can replace some body bits with devices,
like a PACEMAKER that helps your heart beat.
Or a machine outside your body
that cleans your blood,
which is something
the kidneys usually do.

You definitely CAN'T
replace your brain.

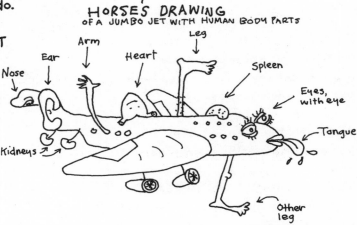

HORSE'S DRAWING
OF A JUMBO JET WITH HUMAN BODY PARTS

Nose
Ear
Arm
Heart
Leg
Spleen
Eyes, with eye
Tongue
Kidneys
Other leg

FACT BOX

The average plane is constructed with zero human body
parts. But ARTIFICIAL LIMBS are made of the same light,
strong metals, plastics and carbon fibre that planes
are made of. And 3D printing is being used to make
replacement cells and even replacement organs, so one
day it might be easier to fix our bodies if we need to.

Lizards can regrow their tails. Salamanders can even regrow parts of their brain. WE can only regrow a few things, like our skin and parts of our liver. And not if they're completely missing.
We can survive, though, if we lose PART of our lungs, for example.
We just don't breathe as well.

Your brain and spinal cord make up your
CENTRAL NERVOUS SYSTEM.

Messages called nerve impulses travel around the body and along the spinal cord between the body and the brain.
NERVE CELLS (sometimes called NEURONS) send and receive electrical signals.

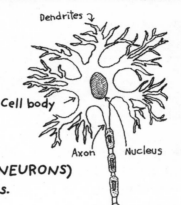

Dendrites

Cell body

Axon   Nucleus

Dendrites: Receive signals from other cells.

Cell body: Keeps the cell working.

Nucleus: Controls the entire neuron.

Axon: transfers signals to other cells and organs.

THE BRAIN

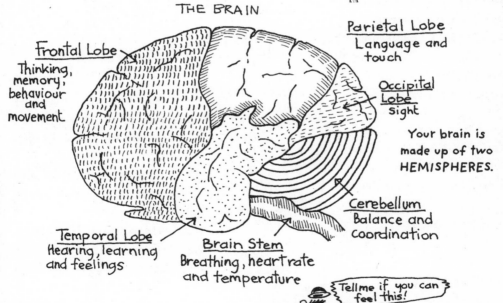

Frontal Lobe
Thinking, memory, behaviour and movement

Parietal Lobe
Language and touch

Occipital Lobe
Sight

Your brain is made up of two HEMISPHERES.

Cerebellum
Balance and coordination

Temporal Lobe
Hearing, learning and feelings

Brain Stem
Breathing, heart rate and temperature

Tell me if you can feel this!

Even PAIN is just an electrical signal.
It's usually a warning that something is wrong.
But it's different for everyone.
And there ARE people who CAN'T feel pain or who feel it all the time.

149

MUSCLES VERSUS FAT

Fat cell

You might think muscles are good and fat is bad.

But FAT cushions and protects your body, and keeps you warm. It also does important jobs, like storing vitamins and energy.

Finding food used to be HARD. You would be grateful for your fat if you didn't eat for a while.

SKELETAL MUSCLE pulls your bones to make them move.

CARDIAC MUSCLE works your heart.

There is SMOOTH MUSCLE around your internal organs.

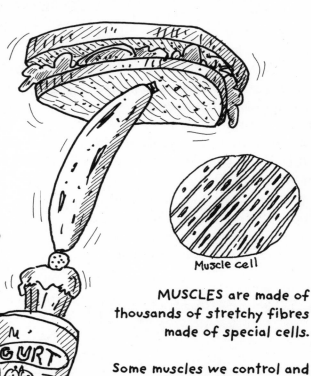

Muscle cell

MUSCLES are made of thousands of stretchy fibres made of special cells.

Some muscles we control and some we don't, like our heart.

Muscles don't just lift things. The little muscles in our face help us show emotion. The biggest muscle is our BUM.

TENDONS attach the muscles to our bones.

Bird!! The artist has mixed up my body parts!

EPIC EVOLUTION FAILS

You probably don't need large fat stores now. And you don't need to be as fit and muscly as ancient humans either.

But there are other body bits that are much less useful.

The APPENDIX hangs around between the small intestine and the large intestine. It probably used to have a job.

I don't know if I'm coming or going.

Just keep turning around until you figure it out.

But it doesn't do anything now, except occasionally burst and have to be removed by a doctor.

The little bones at the end of our spine are the LEAST useful. That's what's left of our ancestors' tail.

FACT BOX

There are lots of cool things we missed out on too. Humans might make maps and read them, but pigeons have a part of their brain that can read the Earth's magnetic field and navigate by it. Snake eyes and brains have an extra bit that detects heat, just like an infrared camera so they can hunt at night. Bees read electrical fields to lead them to flowers. And dolphins and bats use sound beams called SONAR to 'see' what's around them, even in dark water.

YOUR BRAIN IS THE BOSS

Human SPEECH and language are so complex
that they use many areas all over your brain.
Your VOICE BOX in your throat actually makes the sounds.
But one little area on the left hemisphere
of your frontal lobe turns your thoughts into words.

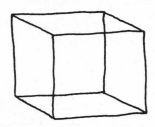

Different parts of the brain make meaning
out of what the senses tell them.
The eyes and brain have
to communicate ESPECIALLY quickly.
OPTICAL ILLUSIONS are when
the brain gets tricked or confused.

Look at this cube for 20 seconds.
Which face seems to be at the
front? Most people see it swap
from one to the other.

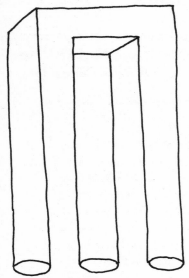

This drawing is
very confusing.
Does it make
sense? Not quite.

It makes my
head ache.

You make my
back ache!

Human brains are pretty big.
Usually about 1.5 kg.
But brain size isn't what makes human brains special.
No one knows exactly what it is.

SIGHT is your super sense.
Your EYES are AMAZING.

Your IRIS is the coloured bit, and the PUPIL controls how much light gets in.

When light travels through ANY curved lens, it flips the image upside-down. That happens in your eye, but your clever brain sorts it out.

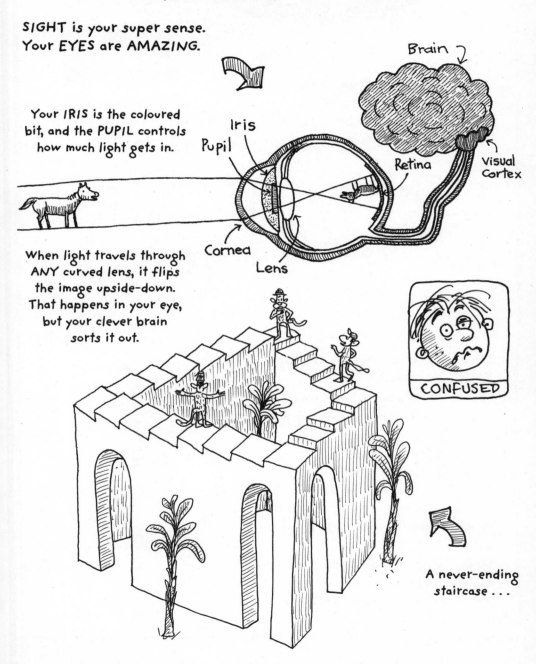

Brain

Iris

Pupil

Retina

Visual Cortex

Cornea

Lens

CONFUSED

A never-ending staircase . . .

FEELING . . .

LIKE A HORSE

When you do something fun,
brain chemicals called
NEUROTRANSMITTERS are released.
They make you feel good, and you smile.

HAPPY

ANGRY

Anger and fear
aren't that different.
There's a special
neurotransmitter for them.

Your automatic reaction to danger is called
FIGHT, FLIGHT, FREEZE.
It was VERY useful back when
people were being chased by aurochs.

You breathe quicker,
your heart beats more.
All your senses are on alert.
All your energy goes
to HELPING YOU SURVIVE.

Unfortunately that reaction can sometimes
happen even if you're NOT in terrible danger.
Then we call it panic or stress.

Your brain does LOADS of things without you knowing.

The brain stem is in charge of ESSENTIAL stuff, like breathing, swallowing, your heart rate and CONSCIOUSNESS.

SLEEPING

Being conscious is being aware of things and reacting to them.

You're not conscious when you sleep. But you might still sleepwalk. And your body is still VERY BUSY growing, repairing, storing memories and dreaming . . .

GOOD DREAM

FLYING

BAD DREAM

FALLING

Dolphins only sleep with half their brain at one time so they can keep swimming.

Horses sleep standing up so they don't become prey.

And birds sleep perched on branches. Their legs lock so they don't fall off.

Sadly we can't do any of that!

Isn't it strange to think that

EVERYTHING

about us, even our thoughts, feelings and personality is because of chemical reactions and electrical signals in our brain?

Sometimes dreams can be so real, it's like you're actually seeing, hearing, touching, tasting and smelling. Even when you're awake, not everyone experiences life the same way.

HEARING is our second-best sense after sight. Sound vibrations travel into your EAR and along the EAR CANAL. They make your EARDRUM vibrate.

Fluid and tiny hairs in this bit move when YOU do. Messages travel up the VESTIBULAR NERVE to the brain to help you balance

In the COCHLEA, sound is converted into signals that go to your brain

OPERA.

NEIGH!

Louder, Horse, I can't hear you.

Outer Ear

Ear Canal

Eardrum

(Bird trying to make Horse hoarse)

Ear hairs

Auditory Nerve (to the brain)

Human skin has lots of nerve endings to tell us about what we TOUCH.

We need to know about things like temperature, pressure and texture and feel things like tickles, itch and pain.

FINGERNAILS ON A BLACKBOARD.

WET DOG SMELL.

FACT BOX

Lots of animals communicate with chemicals called PHEROMONES. They can say A LOT with their stink. That's why dogs leave wee-mails on trees. And how ants can leave a trail to show other ants where the food is. We can't smell most animal pheromones, thank goodness. We have pheromones too, but we don't use them as much.

156

Some people's genes mean they can taste or smell things that others can't. Everyone is different. Your eyes might work well, but the part of your brain that deals with sight might not. If you have SYNAESTHESIA you might see colour when you hear a sound, because two or more parts of your brain are connected up to one sense.

Our noses pick up tiny particles in the air. We're not GREAT at SMELLING compared to animals like sharks. Sharks don't breathe through their nose. It's 100% a smelling MACHINE. And about 2/3 of a shark's brain is about smell.

Mostly, though, people just don't REALISE how important their sense of smell is to them.

STINKY GREEN CHEESE.

FIND THE STINKY GREEN CHEESE TEST

* see below

BRUSSELS SPROUTS.

There are about 10,000 little bumps on your tongue. Those are TASTEBUDS.
We can recognise salt, bitter, sour, savoury and sweet flavours.

But TASTE is made more powerful by being a combination of taste, smell and touch.

* Big shark with hat was correct.
The Stinky Green Cheese was in number 1.

SKIN IS COOL

The outer layer of your skin is waterproof.
It holds in all your squishy bits.

THINGS CARDBOARD-YOU COULDN'T DO . . .

You can't take a shower,

Swim in a pool,

or drink milkshakes.

Your skin is a different texture
to other animals' skin.
And is only about 4 mm thick.
Some whale skin is 35 cm thick.

You shed skin in tiny bits.
Not in one go like a spider.

Your skin cells make a chemical called MELANIN.
That gives you a skin colour.
But octopus skin can match ANY colour,
even though their eyes are colourblind.

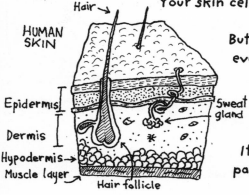

HUMAN SKIN

Hair →

Epidermis

Dermis

Hypodermis →

Muscle layer

Hair follicle

Sweat gland

What human skin IS great
at is SWEATING.
Sweating is stinky, but very useful.
It cools you down so you don't have to
pant or roll in mud like other mammals.

FANCY FEET AND HANDY HANDS

We might not have the sharpest senses of the animal kingdom.
But we have THE MOST AMAZING HANDS.

You can make a strong fist and grab really tightly.
Your clever fingers can do really detailed things
like write and sew and make machines.
They can be strong too.
Some acrobats can balance their whole body
just on their fingers.

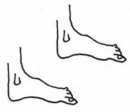

Walking on two legs is HARD.
Your ears, eyes, muscles and brain have to
constantly communicate so you can balance on two feet.

Your short TOES are perfect for running.
And special fat on your heels protects your foot bones.
If our ancestors hadn't walked on two feet,
we wouldn't have evolved our hands.
We would need them to walk on.

```
FACT BOX

A hand is a set of four fingers and an opposable thumb.
Koalas have hands and fingers a lot like ours, but they
have claws, not flat nails. Mostly only primates have hands,
but they often have feet that work like hands too. Other
animals have tails to grasp with, or paws, claws or talons.
```

HAIR, NAILS AND TEETH

The thicker an animal's HAIR or fur
and the OILIER it is
the warmer it will keep them.
Humans have hair nearly everywhere . . .
Except on our palms and the soles of our feet
and our eyelids and lips.
Imagine hairy lips!

Hair falls out and regrows.
It can be so small we don't see it.
Male humans grow a beard,
just like a boy lion grows a mane.
Sadly we don't grow WHISKERS,
which are hairs with special sense powers.

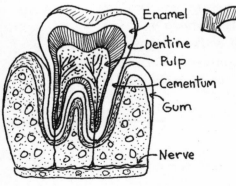

I think I need a haircut, Bird!

Coming!

Hair, FINGERNAILS (and animal horns, claws and hooves)
are all made of keratin.
Hooves are just nails you can stand on.
And claws are curved and SHARP.

Enamel
Dentine
Pulp
Cementum
Gum
Nerve

The outside layer of your TEETH
is the HARDEST THING in your body.
Safe inside the ENAMEL
are the living parts of the tooth.

Stop smiling, Horse.
You know birds have
no teeth!

BEST SMILE
COMPETITION

Humans are omnivores.
So we have a combination of carnivore teeth and herbivore teeth.
Flat MOLARS mush up the food.
Pointy CANINES tear it.
Front INCISORS cut it up.

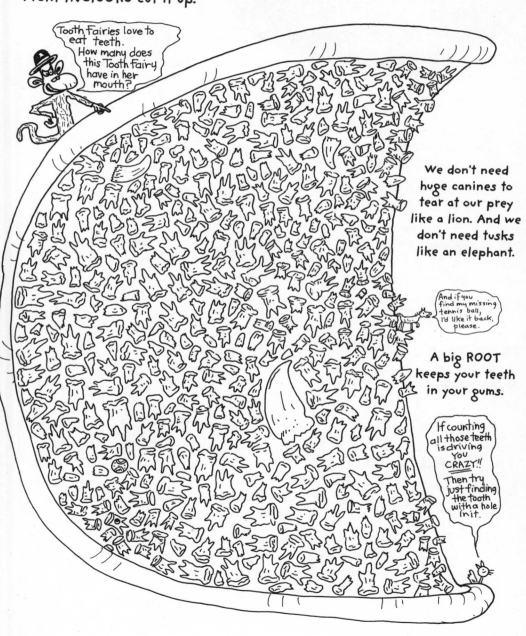

SYSTEMS, ORGANS AND TISSUES

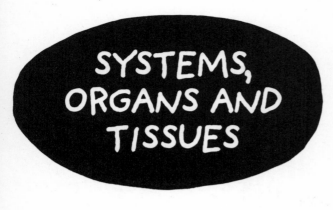

What's inside you, Horse?

I am solid Horse all the way through, Bird.

You already know that we are made up of cells.
But you might not realise how TINY they are.
And that they're not stuck together
in one big PERSON-SHAPED BLOB.

Your cells make up TISSUES (not the kind you sneeze into).

Cells

Tissue

Tissues make up ORGANS (not the kind you play music on).

And organs make up
your body's SYSTEMS.

Musical Organ
(Different to a human organ.)

I've had enough of this stupid body

Spleen

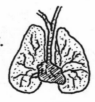

System

Organ

FACT BOX

The main systems of the human body are the circulatory,
digestive and excretory, endocrine, integumentary, immune
and lymphatic, muscular, nervous, renal and urinary,
reproductive, respiratory and skeletal systems.
They all work together to keep us healthy and alive.

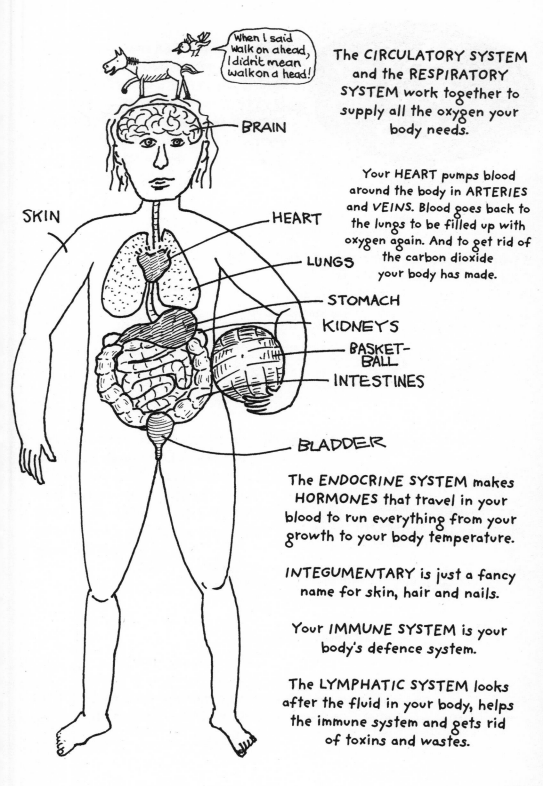

When I said walk on ahead, I didn't mean walk on a head!

BRAIN

SKIN

HEART

LUNGS

STOMACH

KIDNEYS

BASKET-BALL

INTESTINES

BLADDER

The CIRCULATORY SYSTEM and the RESPIRATORY SYSTEM work together to supply all the oxygen your body needs.

Your HEART pumps blood around the body in ARTERIES and VEINS. Blood goes back to the lungs to be filled up with oxygen again. And to get rid of the carbon dioxide your body has made.

The ENDOCRINE SYSTEM makes HORMONES that travel in your blood to run everything from your growth to your body temperature.

INTEGUMENTARY is just a fancy name for skin, hair and nails.

Your IMMUNE SYSTEM is your body's defence system.

The LYMPHATIC SYSTEM looks after the fluid in your body, helps the immune system and gets rid of toxins and wastes.

163

POOS AND WEES

What's funnier than poos and wees? NOTHING is!
Your DIGESTIVE and EXCRETORY SYSTEM is HILARIOUS. And your RENAL and URINARY SYSTEM is pretty amusing too. But do you know how they work?

FOOD IN

POO OUT

A worm's digestive and excretory system is a long tube.
Food goes in one end. Poo goes out the other.
Worms don't have teeth, though, so they have a GIZZARD.
They swallow stones to grind the food up!

FOOD IN

POO OUT

KIDNEY

Blood from body in

Cleaned blood back to body

Waste to bladder

Dogs have teeth and their guts are more complex, but the IDEA is much the same.
And so it is with humans... food in, poo out.
Along the way, some organs take the NUTRIENTS (the useful bits) out of food and others send toxins and wastes out of our body.

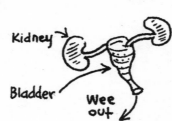

Kidney

Bladder

Wee out

Your kidneys are so important that you have two of them.
They filter your blood and make urine that carries the bad stuff away.

The journey to the stomach is rough.

Food gets chomped by your teeth and sent down the long tube to the guts.

The whole passage is called the ALIMENTARY CANAL.

The stomach prepares the food for digestion by churning it up and adding digestive juices.

Helpful bacteria gets to work. The food becomes a thick paste called CHYME, which enters the small intestine.

Bile and enzymes from your LIVER, GALL BLADDER and PANCREAS break the food down in the small intestine. Molecules of nutrients like amino acids, fatty acids, simple sugars, vitamins and minerals are absorbed into your blood.

In the large intestine more good stuff is absorbed into your bloodstream, including water.

The leftover solid bits, like fibre, are stored in the last section of the large intestine. Have a guess what THEY are. That's right . . .

POOP!

YOU ARE WHAT YOU EAT ...

All life has to make
or eat what it needs to survive.
Energy gets passed along the food chain.
When you eat plants you get the energy they
made from photosynthesis.
When you eat animals and mushrooms you get the energy
THEY got from eating plants and other living things.

Your food is made of carbohydrates, proteins and lipids.
They provide the amino acids, fatty acids, simple sugars,
vitamins and minerals our bodies need.

There are two types of vitamins. You need both.
You've probably heard of Vitamin C. That's a
WATER SOLUBLE vitamin. You can't store it, so you
have to eat fruit and vegetables every day.
The other one is FAT SOLUBLE.
Plants absorb minerals like iron and calcium
from the ground. You can get minerals by
eating plants. You don't have to lick dirt.

CARBOHYDRATES in food give us energy. They are natural (mostly) non-sweet SUGARS.

BREAD

CHEESE

BANANA

FISH

We can store extra energy in two places. For a short time in our muscles and for a long time in fat. Energy storage is why you can survive weeks without food if you have to. But only go a few days without water.

LIPIDS give us FATTY ACIDS that store energy and nutrients (like fat soluble vitamins). They help proteins do their job.

APPLE

MILK

PROTEINS are the most awesomely useful things. There's more than 10,000 different proteins in your body.

Proteins are what cells are MOSTLY made of. And they carry messages and other molecules like oxygen. The type of protein a cell makes decides what job it does.

LAMB
BAAAAD.

MORE BANANAS

FACT BOX

There are healthy foods and unhealthy foods. There are good sugars and fats and bad sugars and fats. The more natural the food, the more useful it is for your body. But some food can carry bacteria or be toxic, or be an ALLERGEN that you have a reaction to.

Viruses are SPECIALISTS in

MAKING US SICK!

There are no virus fossils so we don't know when they first appeared,
but even bacteria can get certain viruses. And viruses evolve FAST.

Remember these disgusting things?
They will make you sick,
maybe even kill you.

Viruses are tiny particles.

They have genes made up
of DNA or something called RNA.

That's disgusting!

AHH-CHOoo!!

They use your cells to reproduce.
They force them to
reproduce more particles OVER and OVER . . .
The virus BURSTS out of one cell and starts attacking others.

VIRUS

Virus releases
RNA into the body
cell.

nucleus

RNA takes over
the nucleus.

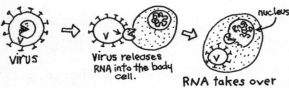

New viral particles
are released. The cell
is destroyed.

Viral RNA uses the
cell to create more
viruses.

So your body works hard
to keep viruses out.
Nose MUCUS and nasal hairs
trap dirt and germs.

Your nose drains into
your stomach so the acid
and helpful bacteria
there can finish germs off.

SPIT kills germs in your mouth.
And salty TEARS wash dirt
or infection out of your eyes.

...heat might kill a vi...   ...and so might soap, by wrecking the fatty layer on their outside. Mostly viruses can't live for very long outside a cell.
Once your body has fought a virus once, you might be IMMUNE.
That's how vaccination works. It teaches your body how to fight a virus you haven't caught yet.

All the yucky things about being sick
are mostly your body trying to help.

Your immune system raises your
temperature to try to fight a germ.
Weirdly that can make you feel COLD and shivery.
But a very high FEVER can be dangerous for you too.

It's just mucus, Horse. It's good for you.

MORE mucus gets rid of MORE germs.
That's why your throat is sore and swollen
and your nose is runny.
You sneeze and cough to get it out.

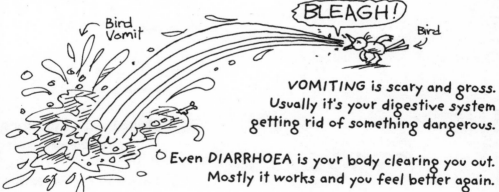

BLEAGH!

Bird Vomit

Bird

VOMITING is scary and gross.
Usually it's your digestive system
getting rid of something dangerous.

Even DIARRHOEA is your body clearing you out.
Mostly it works and you feel better again.

FACT BOX

Sometimes a virus might do so much damage that it's
easy for bad bacteria to settle in. That's when you need
ANTIBIOTICS. Antibiotics CAN'T kill viruses or make
you better faster. They only deal with bacteria. There
ARE medicines called ANTIVIRALS for some viruses.
They don't kill the virus. But they do stop it from
attacking your cells, which is almost as good.

My wing bone is **broken!!**

RED BLOOD CELLS carry oxygen around your body,
and WHITE BLOOD CELLS fight infection.
PLATELETS are a special type of protein in your blood.

If something makes you bleed,
platelets race to the rescue.
They stick together and make a CLOT.
The clot turns into a SCAB on your skin.

Knee grazed!
Knee bleeding!
How will body repair it?!

Pool of knee blood

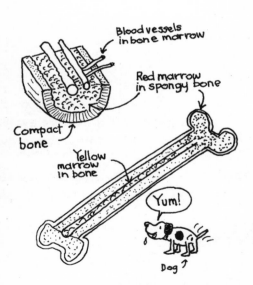

Blood vessels in bone marrow

Red marrow in spongy bone

Compact bone

Yellow marrow in bone

Yum!

Dog ↑

When the skin cells regrow,
the scab will fall off.

A BRUISE is just bleeding
UNDER your skin.

Your body can fix bones too.
It makes a blood clot
around the break.

Then it makes a bony tissue called a CALLUS that gets stronger.
It heals and holds the bone together.

When a mozzie bites you, it sucks your blood
and injects spit that stops your blood clotting!

Why do I have
an itchy lump?

The cells around the bite send out
HISTAMINES,
which call in extra blood and white blood cells.
You might get a red swollen itchy bump.
But if your body overreacts
that's called an ALLERGY.

Why do I have
a bent
proboscis?

Eeeek!

Horses' bottoms
are hard,
that's why!

You might need to take a medicine
called an ANTIHISTAMINE.

Your body can't tell if something is GOOD or BAD.
It just knows that it shouldn't be there.
So even if you NEED a replacement organ
your body might reject it.

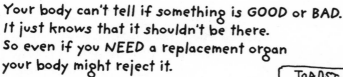

TOADSTOOLS

HAIRY SPIDER

Poisons and venoms attack
the normal ways your body works.
They might attack your nervous system.
Or stop your cells repairing properly.
Or destroy your liver and kidneys
as they try to filter out the bad stuff.

Definite no-nos for lunch.

JAM

CYANIDE
JAM

HAND
GRENADE

TNT

TNT

Not suggested either.

WEIRD BODY FACTS

Bad food . . .
A shooting bean

A bean that's just mean!

We use our senses to figure out if food is okay to eat.
Off food is STINKY.
And we instinctively know that's BAD FOOD.

Bowling ball

But we don't have complex behaviours
that we're born with like other animals.
YOU can't build a nest or a web without being taught.
Humans just have basic REFLEX BEHAVIOURS.
Like being able to grab things as soon as we're born.

Pea

Axe-crazy cucumbers

A pea with TNT

Did you know that, just like flamingos,
if you eat a lot of beta carotene
your skin will turn orange?
That's in carrots and pumpkins.

Asparagus will make your wee smell funny.
And beetroot and berries
can make it go PINK.

But eating lots of sugar doesn't
really make you more energetic.
You're just EXCITED!

Your white blood cells actually 'eat' germs
and damaged and dead cells.
That's what PUS is.
If you pop a pimple, you're pushing extra bacteria
into the new wound you've made.
Pus isn't GROSS. You are!

BIG BAG OF SUGAR

GOOSEBUMPS are the tiny muscles around your body hair tensing up. It used to be useful to fluff up your fur when you were cold or feeling scared.

HICCUPS are spasms in your DIAPHRAGM, the muscle that makes you breathe. It's just above your stomach. You usually hiccup because your stomach is swollen.

I'm coming for your eyelashes.

Eyelash mite ←

MITES are tiny insects. Dust mites eat dead skin cells lying around the house. It's allergy to dust mites, NOT dust, that makes you sneeze.

Most mites that live on human skin feel itchy. But some are see-through and tiny and don't cause trouble. Millions of people don't even NOTICE they have eyelash mites.

A chemical in chilli called CAPSAICIN sets off the nerves in your mouth that detect heat.

Chilli tricks your brain into believing you've been burned. It works on mammals but not on birds.

It can trick the nerves in your skin too. And your eyes. So DON'T TOUCH!

BUCKET of CHILLI

Ooh, look, Bird, horse food.

HORSE FOOD

Those monkeys have gone too far this time!

HORSE FOOD

Stupid Horse!

HA! HA! HA! HA! HA! HA!

Your body is so strange and wonderful. You couldn't make it up if you tried.

5

THE WORLD WE
MADE

YOU'RE SO SMART!

An *INVENTION* is something brand new that someone makes or designs. A *DISCOVERY* is finding something in nature for the first time.

People discovered fire, of course, because it happens in nature.
But MAKING fire was an invention.

Way back before we were Homo sapiens,
someone rubbed two sticks together.
They used the power of friction
to cause combustion.
So now we have other inventions
that rely on combustion
like cars and jet engines.

YOU now know
all the fancy science words
that explain how things work.

Thousands of years ago,
NO ONE knew them
because they hadn't been thought up yet.
But people were still VERY clever.

Cave good!

Fire even better.

I invented sneakers. You're welcome.

For example, 4,000 years ago someone in Central America invented rubber bands and balls, and even rubber shoes.

They used tree sap and a type of vine juice to make rubber for the first time.
So now we have car tyres and gumboots and sneakers.

Discoveries lead to inventions, and one invention leads to another.
Inventors work with what they know about chemistry and the rules of
physics and the power of friction, electricity, magnetism and gravity.

It's just polymer chemistry, mate. No big deal.

Have you heard of a
THERMOPLASTIC RESIN?
The people of ancient Australia hadn't.
But they invented one anyway.

They used resins from grasses to make
a powerful waterproof glue.
It could even attach
stone spearheads to wood.

Because of all the discoveries and inventions,
and people's ability to communicate
and co-operate with each other,
small communities became big communities.

I invented the toga.

About 4,000 years ago,
some SOCIETIES grew to become EMPIRES.
Which meant they ruled over other societies.

Even now, powerful countries try
to build empires with war and trade.

FACT BOX

SOCIETIES are big groups of people living together in
the same area, with the same leadership and language, and
similar cultures and beliefs. A society shares things like a
government and education system, and has family groups
and religions that might be different to other societies.
Some societies are more multicultural than others.

IDEAS ARE INVENTIONS TOO

People in the Middle East started to turn basic symbols into real writing about 6,000 years ago. They wrote their symbols in wet clay. Egyptians created HIEROGLYPHICS at around the same time, but after that they invented something JUST AS IMPORTANT . . .

. . . a type of PAPER!

PAPYRUS was an epic invention.
It was made of reeds. It was light and easy to store.
And better to write on than clay or wood or animal skins.

Then, about 3,500 years ago, a clever trading people called the Phoenicians invented an ALPHABET.

Alphabets are simple to learn because the letters represent SOUNDS not whole words.
You can write ANY word by combining them.
You don't have to learn THOUSANDS of symbols.

A: AARDVARK

About 2,000 years ago,
someone in China
invented paper.

But we had to wait until 1440
to easily print whole books.

A German bloke called
Johannes Gutenberg invented metal letters
that could be arranged and rearranged in a frame.
Each page could be printed many times using a printing press.
Now, of course, we use computers for that!

Thanks to writing, an alphabet, paper and the printing press, you are (almost)
a Professor of Everything. Now you can teach your teacher a thing or two!

I'm so glad books aren't made of animal skins now, Bird.

Me too! They used to write with bird feathers, Horse!

Trained Ninja Mouse

Student

MATHS is another of humanity's
most POWERFUL inventions.

Maths made most of our scientific knowledge and inventions possible.
Lots of ancient number systems were based on our ten fingers.
But about 1,500 years ago, Indian mathematicians invented
PLACE VALUE and ZERO to make everyone's life simpler.

The HINDU-ARABIC DECIMAL SYSTEM makes it much easier to do sums.
And to find the pages in this book.

179

TAKING OVER THE WORLD

As empires got richer and richer and more and more powerful, they developed more complex governments and militaries.

They weren't very nice as they went around their parts of the world conquering other people.

Bird, why don't we go around the world conquering people?

Okay, let's do it.

You might have heard of the ancient Egyptian Empire or the Persian, Greek or Roman empires.
Maybe you know of the Qin or Han dynasty or the Vikings.
None of them lasted.
One would lose power and another one would take over.

But they pretty much invented the MODERN WORLD.

After that, Europeans invented ships that could sail ALL around the world, and the first GLOBAL EMPIRES were born.

FACT BOX

BCE stands for Before Common Era, and CE stands for Common Era. BCE is a bit like negative numbers. 2000 BCE was about 4,000 years ago, for example. In Europe in the Middle Ages people needed a way of keeping track of dates. The Romans were important to them, so the years 1 BCE and 1 CE are both during the Roman Empire. There is no year zero. And for modern dates we drop the CE.

All through history,
people have fought each other
for power or money or land.
Sometimes for religion.
Sadly wars are NOT fought
with pies and rotten fruit.

183

GO NUDE, IT'S NOT RUDE

These days it's the law to wear clothes.
But it wasn't always.
Cultures in warmer areas
didn't really need them.
And ancient people in cold areas only
wore animal skins to stay warm and dry.

Clothes are sometimes part of the rules.
They might protect you from injury at work.
Or be a uniform you HAVE to wear.

Lots of cultures have unique clothes
that are part of their traditional customs.

Sometimes clothes are just
an expression of who you are.

For about 5,000 years, people have
spun wool to make FABRIC.
And cotton, silk and bamboo thread,
can all be woven or knitted together too.

But modern fabrics like nylon and polyester
are made of plastics.
They are called SYNTHETICS.

Early people lived
in caves and sheltered
where they could.

But then they started
to make their own shelters.

Buildings now are made of concrete,
steel, glass, bricks and wood.
But the first homes were made
of natural materials
that were found nearby.

Sometimes they were made of
trees and bark.
Or fabric or animal skins stretched
over wood frames or even whale bones.

Inuit people in Canada built
igloos of blocks of ice.
No wind could get in,
and it was always cosy inside.

Today people might live in a house
or a big apartment block.

Or even on the
International
Space Station.

NOT what the ISS
looks like . . . yet!

MONEY AND TRADE

How much would I sell you for, Horse?

Would you really sell me, Bird?

No, she wouldn't, but I would!

Or barter you for a tasty fly

FOR SALE

Money wasn't always numbers in a bank account.
Or a card you can tap to buy things.
It didn't even start out as coins and notes.

Before money there was BARTER.
If you had a skill, you could trade that for
something you needed, like a chicken.
Once you had a chicken you could exchange eggs
or chicks for other things you needed.

But some ancient people had a clever idea.
They gave things they NEEDED,
like salt or cattle, a set WORTH.
Then they could use them to buy other things.
Some societies even agreed that shells
or marked rocks or cuts on a stick
could be worth something.
When the big empires came along,
they made coins from metal.
One thing hasn't changed since then.
Money is only worth what the society
agrees it's worth.

People exchange skills and time for money.
That's called WORK. You can make and sell things too.

And you can exchange the CURRENCY of one country
for the currency of another country.
One Australian dollar will be worth a certain amount
of British pounds or Japanese yen.
But not always the SAME amount over time.

Countries buy and sell things all the time.
That's called GLOBAL TRADE.

A phone is made up of RAW MATERIALS mined, recycled
or created all around the world.
The raw materials are put together into COMPONENTS
in even more countries.
Those components are SHIPPED
to one country to be put together.
Then the phone goes EVERYWHERE to be sold.
That's a SUPPLY CHAIN.

SPIDER

SPIDER SELFIE

PHONE

SPIDER

FACT BOX

When you buy something from overseas to use or sell it,
that's an IMPORT. When you send it overseas, that's an
EXPORT. Usually you have to pay TAX to the government
to do either of those things. Different countries have
different taxes. A tax is money you pay the government
when you earn money or sometimes when you spend it.

187

EAT YOUR DINNER . . .

These days food is a science. People invented preservatives, tins, glass bottles and vacuum-packed containers so you can store food and never go hungry again.

Cooking food made it easier to digest and killed bad bacteria. But food like cheese and yoghurt have a type of useful bacteria ADDED to them.
And bread rises because we add a fungi called YEAST.

BEAN

COFFEE

POTATO

CHIPS/FRIES

We also cover our food in plastic and add chemicals to change the colour and flavour and texture.

CORN

POP CORN

Plants used to be the only medicine we had.
However . . .
no doctor EVER wrote a prescription for popcorn or chips.

TOMATO

PASTA SAUCE

Momma Janies

Some really terrible sicknesses ARE caused by diets that don't include fresh fruit and vegies.

Like SCURVY,
which is too gruesome to tell you about.
Don't look it up.

AVOCADO

GUACAMOLE DIP

I can't find my head, Horse.

It'll be in that pie somewhere, Bird.

HORSERADISH

WASABI

Pretty much EVERYTHING used to kill you. People died from holes in their teeth and from infected cuts. There was no safe surgery. Not even scans to see what was wrong. And there were no vaccinations to prevent viruses.

SO TAKE YOUR MEDICINE!

The idea of invisible germs spreading between people was thought up by a doctor in the Middle East in 1362. But no one believed it.

I'm a germ and I'm real!

Me, too

I'm sick!

Even 150 years ago, doctors would bleed you with LEECHES, but they wouldn't wash their hands.

My, guts! *Okay, we believe you.*

Drugs found in plants were discovered first. People have been using OPIUM, a painkiller found in poppies, for over 7,000 years.

Now medicines are mostly chemicals made in a lab. But one of the most important medicines was a fungi found by accident.

Penicillin is coming, Horse!!

I think I'm dying, Bird

In 1928, a very messy (but very clever) scientist left a bacteria sample out. When he came back, a mould was eating it up.

That mould was penicillin, the first antibiotic. It saved MILLIONS of lives.

FACT BOX

Over a century ago, a French guy called Louis Pasteur changed how everyone understood germs. He applied his GERM THEORY to food and medicine. Milk is still made safe to drink by going through a process he invented called PASTEURISATION. And remember how vaccines help your immune system to fight a germ without you getting sick? He invented them too.

THE LIFE OF AN EGG

FROM HERE...

THE START

BUK!

Looks like the hen came before the egg.

①

② Your egg is collected with hundreds of others, usually on a BIG conveyor belt.

③ Your egg is washed by a machine and inspected to check it is healthy.

④ Your egg is sorted by weight by a machine in a huge packing factory and placed into a carton.

Maybe the egg gets egg-napped by aliens

Uh, oh?

⑤ Your egg is packed into a big refrigerated truck and travels to a storage centre.

⑥ Your egg travels in a smaller truck to your local shop. It goes on the shelf or in the fridge and waits for you.

Maybe the egg becomes world croquet champ!

Egg →

⑦ You buy your egg at the shop and take it home to fry it.

...TO HERE.

⑧

Z

Yum!

THE END
(OF THE EGG.)

THE LIFE OF A TOMATO

Some food travels huge distances to get to you. Packaged food will always say where it was made, but your fruit and veg might have come from across the seas as well.

MATERIALS AND STUFF

Things MUST be made of the RIGHT STUFF not the WRONG STUFF.
What we can make and invent depends on the MATERIALS we have available.

Helium Horse (cool.)

Lead bird

PAPER AEROPLANE

← leg

Metals and other minerals come from rocks called ORE.
Most are MINED from underground.
Then the ore has to be melted to get the useful bits out.

METALS are shiny and dense.
They conduct electricity and heat and can be magnetic.
We use IRON the most.
When people learnt how useful iron was, it changed our lives SO MUCH that we call that time the Iron Age.

BOWLING-BALL TONGUE PIERCING

But it was mixing iron with other materials to make STEEL that made it so strong.

That's called making an ALLOY.

Steel is EVERYWHERE you look.
From jewellery and appliances to huge machines and frames for buildings.

IRON UNDERPANTS

Things made of the WRONG stuff.

Steel bars are the
RIGHT stuff for
cages. ——→

GRRR

Monkeys
rule.

But we build with CONCRETE the most.
That's a CEMENT PASTE mixed with rocks or sand.
It's hard when it dries.
When it's wet you can pour it
and make it into any shape.

What makes concrete strong, though,
is putting steel rods through it.

LEMON
SPECTACLES

Glass is made of sand.
It's superheated so that it melts.
When it cools again
it's completely different
and very useful.

COTTON-
WOOL
APARTMENT
BLOCKS

It's not just clothes that can be made of chemicals.
PLASTICS are mostly made from FOSSIL FUELS like oil and coal.

ICE-CREAM
SUN

They are so handy because
they are tough and waterproof.
And, unlike metals, they don't carry a current or heat.
Look around and you will probably find something plastic.

Car parts, foam couches and pillows,
toys and clothes, fabrics and carpets,
paint and rope and glue are all made of plastic . . .

FACT BOX

None of these materials are BIODEGRADEABLE.
None of them can be broken down. The heroic
decomposers, the bacteria and earthworms and maggots,
can't eat them and they don't rot. We are stuck with them
forever. But we CAN recycle and reuse them.

FOSSIL FUELS

In the past, societies used people and animal energy to pull and push and lift things.

Horses and oxen and elephants were very useful for that. But elephants aren't MUCH use to us now. Except on washing day.

WASHING MACHINE

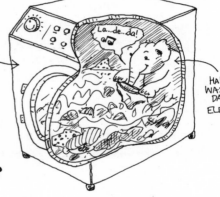

La...de...da!

HAPPY WASHING-DAY ELEPHANT

Most of the energy we use now comes from burning fuel.

Remember how carbon atoms are one of the main ingredients in your body and all life on Earth?

They're also the main ingredient in fossil fuels.

FACT BOX

Fossil fuels take millions of years to be created so we will run out of coal, oil and gas eventually. RENEWABLE energy sources like solar, wind, hydropower and biomass DON'T run out. Sunlight, wind and water are best because they don't add harmful chemicals to the air. Biomass still has to be burned, but we CAN make more of it. It includes wood or a gas or flammable liquid made from animal fat or plants.

Fossil fuels are made of hydrogen and carbon.
COAL is a black rock.
It used to be swampy forests
of prehistoric trees and ferns.

OIL is a black liquid.
It used to be underwater bacteria,
algae and plankton.

NATURAL GAS is mostly methane from
things rotting underground.

Fossil fuels are made when these things
are put under huge pressure for millions of years.

It's the same kind of process that makes DIAMONDS.
But diamonds are a much purer form of carbon.
The GRAPHITE in your pencil is closer to a diamond than coal is.

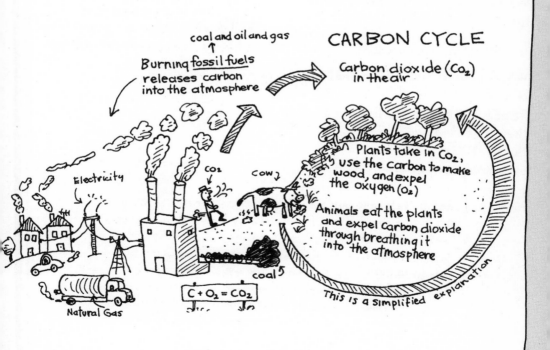

coal and oil and gas

CARBON CYCLE

Burning fossil fuels
releases carbon
into the atmosphere

Carbon dioxide (CO_2)
in the air

Plants take in CO_2,
use the carbon to make
wood, and expel
the oxygen (O_2)

Animals eat the plants
and expel carbon dioxide
through breathing it
into the atmosphere

Electricity

CO_2

cow

coal

$C + O_2 = CO_2$

Natural Gas

This is a simplified explanation

'MAKING' ENERGY

When a piano is pushed up a hill it has the potential energy of the gravity working on it . . .

Energy can't be created (or destroyed).
Remember that fact.
It's important.
AND you sound SMART when you say it.

We don't really MAKE energy
by burning fossil fuels.

We CHANGE one type of energy
into another type.

but when the piano is
pushed off a ledge, the gravitational
energy turns into motion energy.

When people discovered that combustion
is a chemical reaction that
RELEASES energy as light and heat,
they invented ways to turn
the heat part
into movement energy.

Uh, oh!

And used that to POWER our machines.

When the piano hits the ground, the energy goes
into breaking stuff, and turns into other types of
energy, like sound energy.
Because pianos DO NOT bounce.

We don't HAVE to burn fuel to get energy.
We can catch energy that's already in the world.

SOLAR PANELS collect energy
produced by the nuclear reactions in the sun.
They turn it into electrical energy.

WIND TURBINES catch air movement
and turn motion energy into electrical energy.

HYDROPOWER works the same way.
Water is caught behind a dam,
and when it is released the energy moves
a huge turbine that turns it into electrical energy.

A turbine's propellers
catch motion energy and
turn a wheel attached to a
generator.

Pixie energy mostly only
works in toasters,
and only if they are
fitted with flame-
throwers.

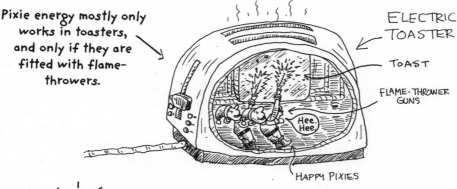

ELECTRIC
TOASTER

TOAST

FLAME-THROWER
GUNS

Hee.
Hee.

HAPPY PIXIES

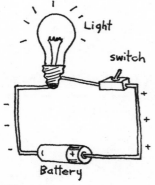

Light

switch

Battery

SIMPLE ELECTRIC CIRCUIT

Batteries don't store ELECTRICITY.
They store potential chemical energy,
which TURNS into electrical energy
when you flick the switch.

ELECTRICAL WIRES are made of
a metal that conducts well.
The electricity passes through easily.

The wires are covered in plastic,
which DOESN'T conduct.
That keeps the electricity in and keeps you safe.

MARVELLOUS MACHINES

Remember gravity, magnetic force and friction,
the forces working on everything all the time?
They allow us to move and slow and turn and fall.
And they can stop us from doing those things too.

Simple machines APPLY force to make doing things EASIER.

load

↓ Force

Used to lift loads.

LEVER

Or to fling people high in the air.

WHEEL and AXLE

Turn the axle and the wheel turns.

Wheels and axles are used for
movement, lifting things
and producing energy we can use.

SCREW

Screws tighten
and join, drill,
lift or move. They
can even be used to
pump liquids.

WEDGE

Wedges lift, split, cut and tighten.
Used differently, a wedge becomes
an INCLINED PLANE.

PULLEY

↓ Force

Load

Pulleys lift and pull.

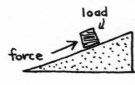

load

force

The
Egyptians
used these
in their
pyramid
building.

Levers MULTIPLY force.

The further you are from the FULCRUM of a lever
the more your force is magnified.

A seesaw, a crowbar
and a pair of scissors are levers.
There are levers in wheelbarrows
and bottle openers, piano keys
and brakes on trains.

A lever
at work

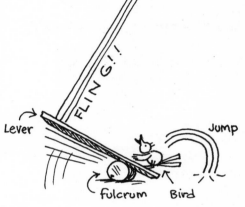

Horse

FLING!!

Lever

Jump

Fulcrum   Bird

All COMPLEX MACHINES
are made up of simple machines
with extra parts added.

A car and its engine are just
thousands of simple machines
all working together.

A SPRING stores and releases energy so it can do our bouncing for us.

Zigmund travels by Belly-button bounce-a-matic.

These days complex machines like computers can even do our THINKING for us.

COMPUTERS store and process data. They take information in, and follow the instructions that are written in their PROGRAM.

Then they OUTPUT the new information.

Maisie travels by Genetically engineered leg springs.

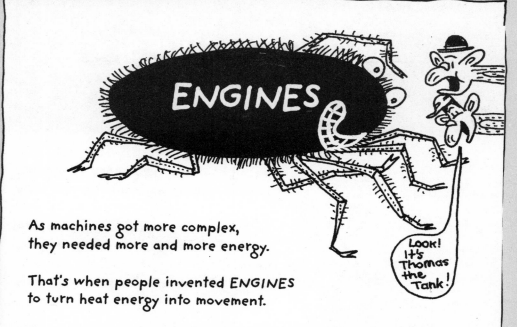

ENGINES

As machines got more complex,
they needed more and more energy.

That's when people invented ENGINES
to turn heat energy into movement.

The first really powerful engines were STEAM ENGINES.
They ran fast trains and BIG machines in factories.

STEAM ENGINE

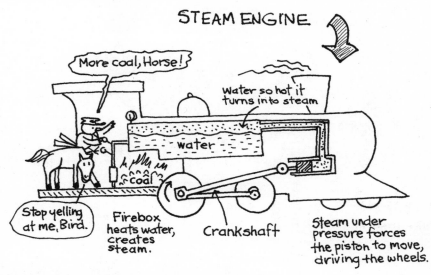

Burning coal boiled water and created steam.
The pressure of the steam pushed a piston
backwards and forwards.
That moved a crankshaft that turned a wheel.

MORE ENGINES!

You might think the science of engines is hard to understand. But it's not really.

Engines that run on petrol lose LESS energy than steam engines because the fuel is burned *INSIDE* the cylinder. That reaction drives the piston directly.

That's why they're called *INTERNAL COMBUSTION ENGINES.*

YAY!!

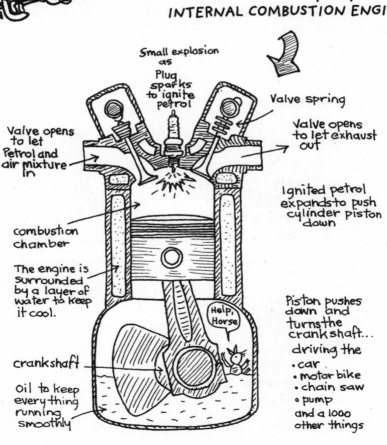

Small explosion as Plug sparks to ignite petrol

Valve spring

Valve opens to let Petrol and air mixture in

Valve opens to let exhaust out

Ignited petrol expands to push cylinder piston down

combustion chamber

The engine is surrounded by a layer of water to keep it cool.

Help, Horse

Piston pushes down and turns the crankshaft...

driving the
• car
• motor bike
• chain saw
• pump
and a 1000 other things

crankshaft

oil to keep everything running smoothly

Steam engines were a HUGE step forward. But lots of the energy was released as light instead of heat. And it took a lot of heat energy to boil the water, so they used up a LOT of coal.
People needed BETTER ENGINES.

Rockets and planes use JET ENGINES.
A chemical reaction shoots jets of gas behind them.

That pushes them forward
VERY FAST.

Some big ships and submarines
are NUCLEAR POWERED.

They SPLIT atoms of uranium
to create heat.
That's called FISSION.

It's also how the nuclear bomb works.
Fission doesn't burn anything,
but you have to be very careful.
Even if you don't EXPLODE,
the leftover bits from the reaction
are RADIOACTIVE and can kill you.

FACT BOX

After a while, people stopped powering their machines with steam engines and used MOTORS that ran on electricity instead. In the motor, electrical energy from the wall socket turns into movement energy to run appliances like washing machines or the wheels of an electric car. Coal IS still burned to make steam, though. It's just happening somewhere else in a massive power plant where the steam is used to produce electricity.

WHEELY, WHEELY GOOD

For a VERY long time, people got around by walking. And sometimes running when there was a lion about.

But then they got sick of walking and running so they invented the skateboard.

The first skateboards were made of stone.

Actually, it didn't QUITE happen like that...

In about 3500 BCE, a human invented a wheel.

Cave man

Antelope

Riding around on one wheel was not much fun, so eventually humans invented the SECOND wheel.

What it for, Zog?

STILL NOT SO USEFUL until someone called AXLE* invented a machine. It was a bit of wood to join the two wheels. He called it an AXLE.

*Latest research suggests he MIGHT not have been called Axle. He might not even have been a he. It really is called an axle, though.

This heaps good, Zog.

When a strong axle made of metal was combined with the wheel, people really got moving . . .

Faster . . .

And faster . . .

And FASTER . . .

AND THEN SLOWER...

In about 2000 BCE, the spoked wheel was invented and was used in chariots pulled by horses.

In 1886, the first car (automobile) was invented when a petrol engine was added to a three-wheeled cart.
It could only go about 16 km per hour, but WHEEL + ENGINE = CAR
And now the fastest car has a top speed of 435 km per hour.

And the slowest one is the one sitting in a traffic jam.

TAKE OFF!

The wheel was actually first invented to make pottery, not move us around. We'd even invented the flute before the wheel. Thankfully someone figured it out.

The first planes might have looked like birds . . .

but they didn't fly.

THESE didn't fly either.

THIS was what the first powered aircraft looked like.

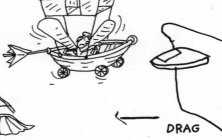

DRAG

The first powered flight was in 1903.
Two American brothers put a light engine on a glider.
It flew for 12 seconds and travelled 37 m.

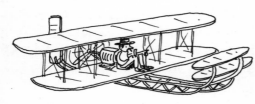

But look what we have now...

We use wheels and axles as tiny gears in watches and to generate electricity with massive turbines. Even a doorknob and a screwdriver turning a screw is a type of wheel and axle. Without wheels we wouldn't have bikes or cars, and we wouldn't have planes . . .

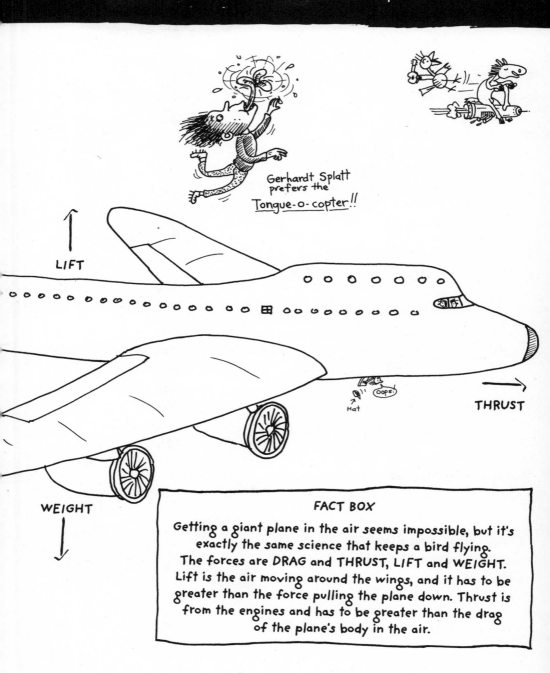

Gerhardt Splatt prefers the Tongue-o-copter!!

LIFT

THRUST

Hat

Oops!

WEIGHT

FACT BOX

Getting a giant plane in the air seems impossible, but it's exactly the same science that keeps a bird flying.
The forces are DRAG and THRUST, LIFT and WEIGHT.
Lift is the air moving around the wings, and it has to be greater than the force pulling the plane down. Thrust is from the engines and has to be greater than the drag of the plane's body in the air.

207

Our body systems keep our bodies
running. And our cities have
systems too.
Mostly they're invisible.
You won't notice them
until they go WRONG.

CITY SYSTEMS

There are SEA ROUTES for boats
and HUGE container ships.

There are AIR ROUTES
that act like roads in the sky for planes,
as well as giant eagle flights
and light earwing and pelican transport.*

Bob travels by EARWINGS.

Ear
wings.

Suction cups
to assist
landing on
the side of a
building.

Giant
eagle.

By pelican.

I travel by
magical wing power.

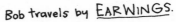

Very powerful
guinea-pig
power.

TRANSPORT and ROAD SYSTEMS
help us travel around safely
on the ground.

Tortoise power.

*Some modes of transportation mentioned here are not based on TRUE FACT.

Imagine if the SEWERAGE SYSTEM didn't magically carry away our used household water and the poopy toilet water.

What if it didn't go to a FILTRATION PLANT to be cleaned before it ran into the sea?

Imagine if the STORMWATER SYSTEM didn't make sure the streets don't flood.

Or if pipes underground didn't bring clean water and natural gas for cooking and heating.

The system you use the most is the ELECTRICITY GRID.

Electric current flows from the power station to your street and through wires into your house so you can turn on the light.

I can remember when our house wasn't full of Poo, Bird

My jelly's battery has gone flat.

Lots of marine animals can create their own light. They have cells called PHOTOPHORES that make light with chemicals or bacteria.

We can't do that. So we had to invent the light bulb.

FACT BOX

TELECOMMUNICATION is communication at a distance by electrical signals or electromagnetic waves. These days that could mean telephone, radio, tv or the internet. The INTERNET is a network of special computers all around the world. They move information around so you can pretend to know EVERYTHING.

LET THERE BE LIGHT!

I love Tungsten filament lights the best.

The **LIGHT BULB** is one of the most important inventions of ALL TIME.

If you look inside a light bulb you'll see a thin wire. That's what lights up.

ELECTRICAL CURRENT is the flow of electrons. They are flowing along the wire from the – terminal to the + terminal. But they are NOT flowing EASILY. The wire is made of a different metal to the one used in electrical wires.

Because there's RESISTANCE, the wire is heating up and glowing.

You're ACTUALLY watching electrical energy turning into heat and light energy. Amazing, isn't it?

Glass globe

Tungsten filament

Metal base

Electrical connection

LIGHT BULB

And the bulb isn't full of air. There's a different gas in there to make sure the wire doesn't react with oxygen when it gets hot.

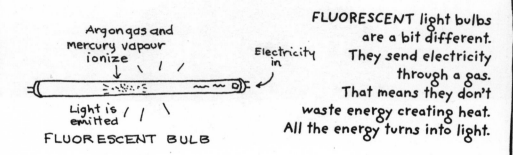

Argon gas and mercury vapour ionize

Electricity in

Light is emitted

FLUORESCENT BULB

FLUORESCENT light bulbs are a bit different. They send electricity through a gas. That means they don't waste energy creating heat. All the energy turns into light.

Lots of lights now are LEDs.
LED stands for LIGHT EMITTING DIODE.

Any screen is just tons of LEDs put together. So are traffic lights, digital watch faces and almost all electronics.

LED LIGHT

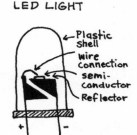

Plastic Shell
Wire connection
semi-conductor
Reflector

+   -

Moths like light, so I like lights.

CRUNCH!

A light meal

LEDs are tiny. They are made of something called a SEMI CONDUCTOR MATERIAL. It reacts when electricity goes through it. And different chemicals give you different colours.

Tungsten! They're rubbish. LED lights up my life!

FACT BOX

You can only watch TV because over a thousand tiny LEDs in your screen light up to make a picture. Lots of slightly DIFFERENT pictures flash in front your eyes, and that tricks your brain into seeing movement. It's just like making a stop motion animation.

It's hard to imagine
a time before phones,
so here are some instructions
to make your own.

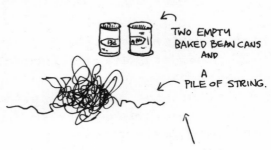

TWO EMPTY
BAKED BEAN CANS
AND

A
PILE OF STRING.

Put a hole in the ends
of the cans (see diagram 1).
Thread one end of the string
through the hole in Can #1.

Can #1   CAN #2

one end
solid

one end
open

DIAGRAM 1

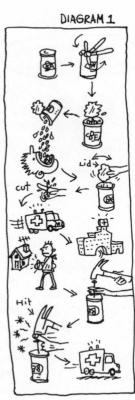

← Matchstick

Tie a knot around an old matchstick.

Hole

matchstick

And pull the string tight.
Do the same with Can #2.

can #1

can #2

COMMUNICATE!

You can hold Can #1 and get your friend* to hold Can #2.
Now walk away from each other until the string is tight.
There are two possibilities from here.

Possibility #1 You are standing a long way away
from each other.

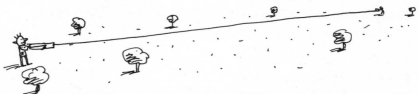

Possibility #2 You are standing very close to one another.

So, you need to untangle the strings.

NOW hold Can #1 up to your mouth and talk.
Your friend* holds Can #2 up to their ear and listens.

Your voice is just air being pushed through your
VOICE BOX in your throat.
It makes your VOCAL CORDS vibrate.
That causes sound vibration in the air,
which causes vibration in the tin can.
The sound energy continues to vibrate through the string!

*Or someone else's friend or your dog.

213

Before tin cans, you had to send a
letter to communicate long distance,
or make smoke signals or coded drumbeats.
Or keep trained pigeons with
little notes strapped to their legs.

Tin cans were invented in the year 1810
to preserve food, not make calls.

Thankfully, soon after that the TELEGRAPH was invented.

MORSE CODE was a code that sent messages around the world
using a combination of short and long electrical pulses.
They were known as DOTS and DASHES.

A	·−	J	·−−−	S	···	1	·−−−−
B	−···	K	−·−	T	−	2	··−−−
C	−·−·	L	·−··	U	··−	3	···−−
D	−··	M	−−	V	···−	4	····−
E	·	N	−·	W	·−−	5	·····
F	··−·	O	−−−	X	−··−	6	−····
G	−−·	P	·−−·	Y	−·−−	7	−−···
H	····	Q	−−·−	Z	−−··	8	−−−··
I	··	R	·−·	0	−−−−−	9	−−−−·

The messages were called TELEGRAMS.
Ships, planes and emergency services all used Morse Code.
Messages could be sent by radio or along telegraph wires.

FACT BOX

In any communication there is a TRANSMITTER that
changes the message into something that can travel
(called a SIGNAL). There's a medium the signal can
travel along, called a CHANNEL, and a RECEIVER at the
other end to change the message back to something we
understand. Sometimes a device can be both a transmitter
and a receiver.

Some radiation can be dangerous. But other types of radiation are around you all the time. Remember how light is part of the electromagnetic spectrum?

Light is the part of the electromagnetic spectrum we can see. Other types of electromagnetic radiation include microwaves, x-rays and RADIO WAVES.
All of them are really useful.

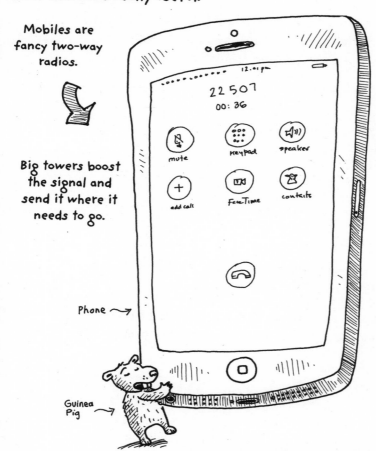

Mobiles are fancy two-way radios.

Big towers boost the signal and send it where it needs to go.

Phone →

Guinea Pig →

12.01 pm

22 507
00: 36

mute   keypad   speaker

add call   FaceTime   contacts

Your voice or your text is converted to electrical signals and travels through the air using radio waves.

Satellite phones send their signal into space to bounce off a satellite.

Not long ago, how we communicate today would have seemed like MAGIC. Not SCIENCE.

6

TIME FLIES

HAVE YOU GOT THE TIME?

When you were a baby you had heaps of time.
You've still got ages now.
But as you get older it feels like you have *less* and *less* time to spare.
There's more and more you HAVE to do.
And more and more you're ABLE to do.

When time goes slow, then we can get bored.
When time goes fast, then we can get exhausted.

Time flies when you're having fun.
It flies the fastest when you don't want to get out of bed.

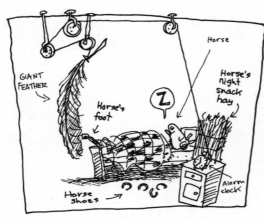

GIANT FEATHER

Horse's foot

Horse

Horse's night snack hay

Z

Horse shoes

Alarm clock

HORSE HAS A SPECIAL ALARM CLOCK. BECAUSE HE HAS TO SLEEP WITH EAR-MUFFS HE DOESN'T HEAR THE ALARM. SO HE HAS A GIANT FEATHER* WHICH WOBBLES WITH THE ALARM AND TICKLES HIS FOOT.

* THE TINY GIANT FEATHER BIRD
Giant feathers come from a very tiny bird WITH A VERY LONG TAIL with just ONE feather.

There's no way we know to stop time, though.

TIME IS SO IMPORTANT THAT WE TALK ABOUT IT ALL THE TIME...

Time after Time
Time and a half
Time and time again
Time bomb
Time flies
Time honoured
Time release capsule
Serving time
Time catching up
Time the great healer
On time
Timetable
Good time
Bad time

TIME ISN'T JUST HOW IT FEELS

For tens of thousands of years and in every culture across the world, people have tried to chop time up and order it using clocks and calendars.

A SUNDIAL
As the Sun moves across the sky it casts a shadow across numbers.
So the position of the Sun gives you the time of day.
Not so good at night or on a cloudy day.

THE STARS
Through the night the stars appear to rotate around the poles, so you can tell the time by the position of the stars.
No good for daytime.

AN HOURGLASS
Sand falls from the top glass to the lower one through a small hole.
Good for short periods of time, a day maybe, but any longer and you need a HUGE hourglass.

AN EGYPTIAN WATER CLOCK
A bit like the hourglass, except with water not sand. It could be used to mark the time through several days.
It can be big, though, so it's not easy to carry around.

Modern clocks are different. They all work by counting the TICKS or PULSES of something that's moving or changing.

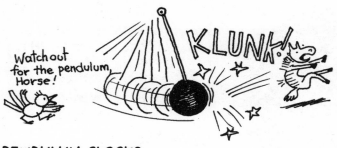

Watch out for the pendulum, Horse!

KLUNK!

Time to run!

PENDULUM CLOCKS
In 1656, clocks were invented that counted the ticks of a swinging weight. They were the first really accurate clocks.

MECHANICAL CLOCKS
After the development of metal springs and gears, clocks counted the swings of a little balance wheel inside. It works well so long as you wind it.

Annoying Alarm clock

RING!!

QUARTZ CLOCKS
They count vibrations from a quartz crystal inside the clock. First built in 1927 and very accurate. Can be DIGITAL or ANALOG.

DIGITAL CLOCKS
Battery-driven digital clocks have replaced most other methods of telling the time. The time on your phone is based on the signal from a GPS satellite orbiting the Earth.

ATOMIC CLOCKS
About 400 atomic clocks all work together to figure out UTC. They measure the time it takes for a caesium atom to change back and forth between two states. Confused? That's okay. It's VERY complicated!

FACT BOX

After 1847, GREENWICH MEAN TIME (GMT) was the standard time that everyone set their clocks to. Now COORDINATED UNIVERSAL TIME (UTC) is the international standard. Having a standard time means we can all agree what time it is on the International Space Station or on a plane. UTC isn't affected by daylight saving time or time zones.

Your TIME ZONE tells you the time where you are RIGHT NOW.
It's based on how far you are from Coordinated Universal Time (UTC).

The UK is in the 'middle' of the map and uses UTC
because they came up with the idea in 1880.

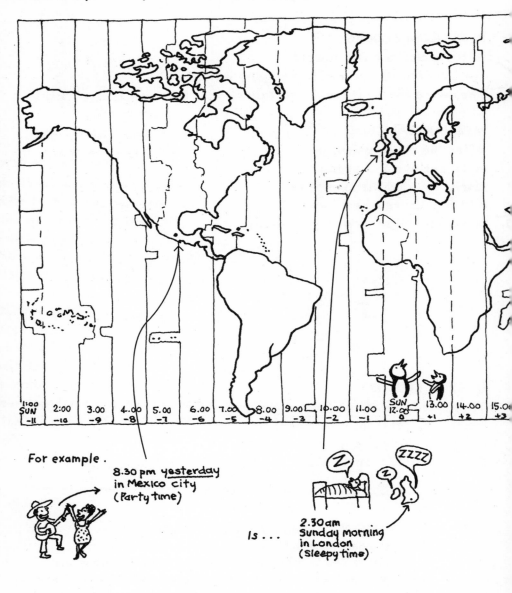

| 1:00 SUN | 2:00 | 3.00 | 4.00 | 5.00 | 6.00 | 7.00 | 8.00 | 9.00 | 10.00 | 11.00 | SUN 12.00 | 13.00 | 14.00 | 15.00 |
| -11 | -10 | -9 | -8 | -7 | -6 | -5 | -4 | -3 | -2 | -1 | 0 | +1 | +2 | +3 |

For example.

8.30 pm yesterday
in Mexico city
(Party time)

Is . . .

2.30 am
Sunday morning
in London
(sleepy time)

Imaginary lines run from pole to pole, and countries are either 'ahead' or 'behind' UTC, depending on where they are on the map.

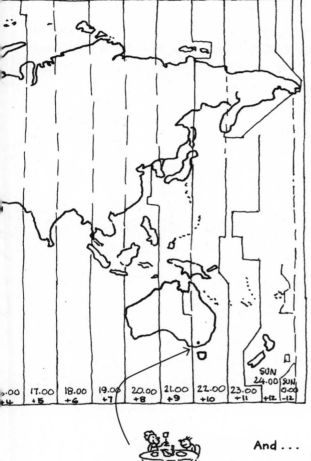

Most clocks split 24 hours into 12 hours of AM and 12 hours of PM.

But some clocks use 24-HOUR TIME. This means you count the hours from zero to 23.

It's easy to read 24-hour time.

For all the hours after midday, you just add 12. So the school bell goes at 3.30PM, which is the same as 15:30 (because 3 + 12 = 15).

| ..00 | 17.00 | 18.00 | 19.00 | 20.00 | 21.00 | 22.00 | 23.00 | SUN 24.00 | SUN 0.00 |
| +4 | +5 | +6 | +7 | +8 | +9 | +10 | +11 | +12 | -12 |

And ...

Sunday in Melbourne at 1.30pm (Lunch time)

FACT BOX

DAYLIGHT SAVING TIME is when clocks are changed to give us an extra hour of daylight on summer evenings. You put your clock forward by an hour in spring (when the days start to get longer), and back again to the usual time in autumn. Not all countries choose to use daylight saving time. Sometimes not even all states in the same country use it.

CALENDARS

Most societies based their calendars on what they could see in the sky — the cycles of the Moon (months) or the movement of the Sun (years).

So there are LUNAR CALENDARS or SOLAR CALENDARS. One of the earliest lunar calendars is in Scotland. It's about 10,000 years old and it's HUGE.

That calendar won't fit in the pocket... it's 50 metres long!

Haggis

Spare haggis

The different shapes of the moon are big pits dug into the ground

— 50 m —

The ancient Babylonians could see the Sun, the Moon, Mercury, Venus, Mars, Jupiter and Saturn in the sky so they liked the number seven. And created a seven day week.

We also use their idea of 60 seconds and 60 minutes.

This is the only way to blow bagpipes.

These Scotch Eggs are sure hard to hatch.

Our counting system is based on tens, but 4,000 years ago theirs was based on 60. Imagine remembering your times tables back then!

After 1582, most of the world used the GREGORIAN CALENDAR.
That's MOSTLY a solar calendar,
but it's clever because it includes a LEAP YEAR.

There are 365 days in our calendar year,
but remember how it takes about 365.25 days
for us to orbit the Sun?

He was born on February 29

That means I only have a birthday every 4 years! So unfair!

Every four years we add an extra day
(February 29) to line up the calendar
with the solar year.

Just to confuse you, our months DON'T match
the cycles of the Moon as we see them from Earth.
It's about 29.5 days before we see the full Moon again,
but our months have 31 or 30 days (except February, of course).

Hey, Julius. Let's make sure this calendar make **no sense** at all.

Our 12 months are based on
a Roman calendar from 46 BCE.
It only had 10 months to start with.
So the Romans added two months,
but at the BEGINNING of the year.

That's why the ninth month, September,
actually means the 'seventh' month in Latin.
And October, November and December
mean 'eighth', 'ninth' and 'tenth'.
Nice one, Romans!

FACT BOX

The Gregorian calendar is the official calendar used all
around the world, but there are six other calendars also in
use — the Chinese, Hebrew, Islamic, Persian and Ethiopian
calendars and the Balinese Pawukon. If you find a leap year
confusing, imagine using a lunar calendar. You'd need to add
a 13th month every few years to catch up.

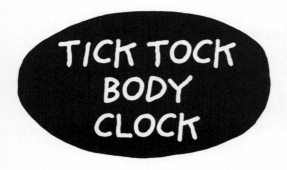

TICK TOCK BODY CLOCK

Living things have natural rhythms that repeat every 24 hours. They're called CIRCADIAN RHYTHMS. They're controlled by BODY CLOCKS.

Plants have them, animals have them. GIANT SPIDERS have them. Even fungi and bacteria have a body clock.

It tells them when to be energetic or grow and when to sleep or eat.

It organises the rest of the body's systems to help.

I got circadian rhythm, Bird!

It may be circadian, Horse, but it's certainly not rhythm.

It even knows the best time to fight infection, heal a wound or digest food. That's daytime, so midnight snacks are out!

A part of your brain with an EXTREMELY complicated name sends out chemical signals to all the different parts of your body.

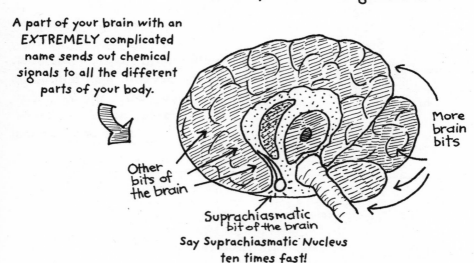

More brain bits

Other bits of the brain

Suprachiasmatic bit of the brain

Say Suprachiasmatic Nucleus ten times fast!

Plants 'breathe', but only at night.
Some mushrooms glow in the dark to attract bugs,
but they don't waste their energy by glowing during the day.
And your pets might be waiting at the door when you get home,
but they haven't checked the clock.

Even eyeless cave fish that have evolved in the dark can tell time.
But after two million years without sunlight their body clock
is 47 hours long, not 24.

Birds migrate at the same time each year.
Other animals put food away for winter.
Jumping spiders (which are very clever) can plan ahead, make a
mental map and follow it to sneak up on their prey (SHUDDER!)
Other animals remember and learn,
but do they have a history or personal memories?
We don't know.
Maybe that's unique to humans.

FACT BOX

Your body clock can get messed up by things like artificial
light, screen time or staying up all night. JET LAG is what
happens when our body clock and the local time disagree.
When you cross time zones, the clock might say it's 2AM,
but your body says it's LUNCHTIME. Luckily you can retrain
your body clock to fit the new times.

GIANT SPIDERS
THROUGH TIME

NEANDERTHAL GIANT SPIDER

THE STONE AGE
(until about 3000 BCE*)

Invented fire, language, music, clothing, fabric and buildings, stone and wood tools and weapons, art and pottery wheels, boats, farming and domestic animals, clocks and calendars, basic writing, counting and currency. Not a bad start!

STONE AGE GIANT SPIDER

*BCE Before common era

Fly

THE BRONZE AGE
(3000 BCE until about 1200 BCE)

Metal made everything easier. Invented metal tools, weapons, jewellery and pots, proper wheels and chariots, pulleys, soap, umbrellas, writing, papyrus and towns. Improved on all the Stone Age stuff.

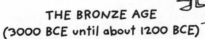

E.g. the Egyptian Empire

THE IRON AGE
(1200 BCE until about 650 CE*)

Invented oars, big ships and coins.

Plus, iron made almost everything better, especially farming tools, transport and weapons. It was NOT better if you were at the wrong end of a sword or an arrow, though.

EGYPTIAN GIANT SPIDER

*CE Common era

Giant spiders found out more about their history when archaeologists dug up things from their past. Ancient giant spiders were often buried with the things that were important to them, so historians could tell from that how they lived and what they valued.

E.g. the Greek Empire

CLASSICAL GREEK
GIANT SPIDER

← Stick

E.g. Qin and Han Dynasty China

CHINESE
TERRACOTTA
WARRIOR
GIANT SPIDER

E.g. the Roman Empire

ROMAN GIANT SPIDER
200 BCE

THE MIDDLE AGES
(between about 500 CE
and 1450 CE)

E.g. the Viking Age

10th CENTURY
VIKING GIANT SPIDER

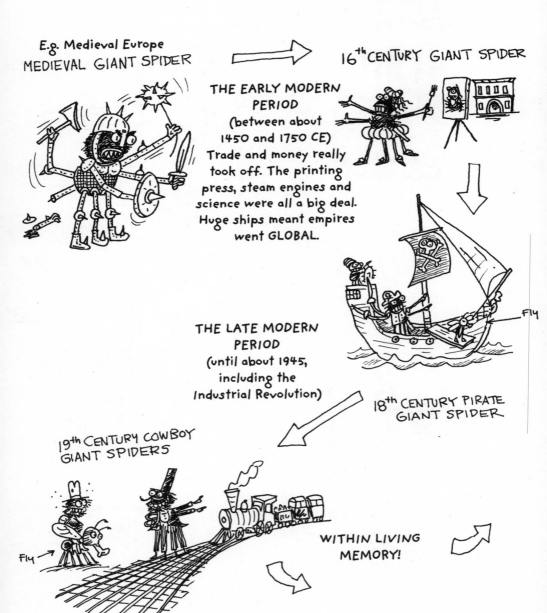

E.g. Medieval Europe
MEDIEVAL GIANT SPIDER

16th CENTURY GIANT SPIDER

THE EARLY MODERN PERIOD
(between about 1450 and 1750 CE)
Trade and money really took off. The printing press, steam engines and science were all a big deal. Huge ships meant empires went GLOBAL.

THE LATE MODERN PERIOD
(until about 1945, including the Industrial Revolution)

Fly

18th CENTURY PIRATE GIANT SPIDER

19th CENTURY COWBOY GIANT SPIDERS

Fly →

WITHIN LIVING MEMORY!

More recent giant spider history is written down and recorded. A PRIMARY SOURCE is something created at the time by the people who lived through the experience. A SECONDARY SOURCE is created by someone based on primary sources.

20ᵗʰ CENTURY ROCK'N'ROLL GIANT SPIDER

21ˢᵗ CENTURY OFFICE WORKER GIANT SPIDER

NOW!

Office Worker

Scratch

Hello. Hello

THE FUTURE — the great unknown!

22ᴺᴰ CENTURY SPACE GIANT SPIDER

FACT BOX

You might have noticed that lots of important things like farming and domestication, happened for the first time about 10,000 years ago during the Stone Age. That's called the NEOLITHIC REVOLUTION. Neolithic stone tools were better made and smoother than before. The period before the Neolithic is called the PALEOLITHIC STONE AGE.

LOOKING INTO THE PAST

Leonardo de Spider

Okay, so MAYBE that was the history of
PEOPLE, not giant spiders.
Other than that it's all true.

PREHISTORY is the time before writing.
People could remember and share stories
but they couldn't record them.

Early written history is not all that accurate.
Two of the MOST FAMOUS historical stories,
THE ILLIAD and THE ODYSSEY, were
(probably) first written down in Ancient
Greece
between 700 and 800 BCE. But the events are
(probably) from much earlier.

The author was (possibly) a bloke called Homer
or (possibly) a group of people.
The stories were (probably) a collection of
much older poems and songs that had been
helping people to remember their history
long before writing existed.

But stories from these books are still being told
and retold. You might know about the Greek
God Zeus, or the story of
the Trojan Horse.

UGH!

BIRD 10,000
YEARS AGO

HORSE
IN HIS
EGYPTIAN
PAST LIFE

THE AUTHOR
AS A
NEANDERTHAL
ARTIST

(239)

Those Giant Spiders are back, Bird!

Be afraid, Horse.

The very earliest artworks are drawings in caves and on rock walls.

Some were created about 35,000 years ago. They are pictures of animals and even people, as well as outlines of handprints.

IT'S THAT STUPID GIANT SPIDER AGAIN!

He's got to go!

233

BACK TO THE FUTURE!

We only know so much about prehistoric animals and plants because they left fossils behind.

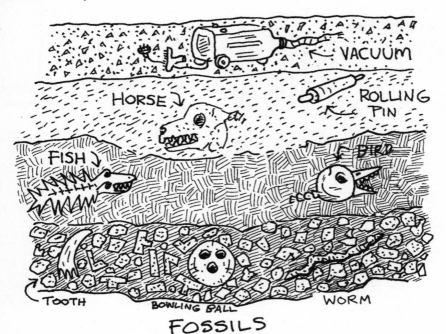

VACUUM

HORSE ↓

ROLLING PIN

FISH ↓

BIRD

TOOTH

BOWLING BALL

WORM

FOSSILS

Something is considered a fossil if it's over 10,000 years old. The oldest are about 3.5 billion years old. How many of these buried things are really fossils?*

*NONE. They were all buried AFTER the invention of the bowling ball in 1862.

How to become a fossil. Be dead. Be buried immediately. Sand or mud is best. Wait two million years while minerals turn your bones to stone. Be discovered. Voilà!

PETRIFIED WOOD is a fossilised tree.
It looks like it used to,
but it is VERY old, VERY hard
and now made of rock.

Now I'm going to be late for dinner... by about 100million years...

AMBER

The oldest **AMBER FOSSIL**
is 320 million years old.
Creatures trapped in amber,
the gooey sap of ancient trees,
were perfectly preserved.

Tell me about it !!

They look just like they did
when they were alive.

The past was the future once.
One day all the things in YOUR life will be history.

But you don't have to wait two million years,
turn to stone and get dug up as a fossil.

You can make a TIME CAPSULE.

What's in it?

I am, Bird!

A time capsule is a sealed
container full of things
worth remembering — your
treasures or messages or
drawings, or information
you think the future needs
to know.

There's even a time capsule on the Moon, put there by the Apollo 11
astronauts. It's a disc about the size of a 50 cent coin.
It has tiny messages engraved on it from world leaders.
On the front it says, 'We came in peace for all mankind'.

HOW LONG HAVE YOU GOT?

At best people only get about 100 years of alive time. And that's actually pretty good for a mammal.

GIANT SPIDER AT 5

" 🕷 "

Huon pines in Tasmania can live for 3,000 years, and lots of plants can live for hundreds of years.
Some whales and fish can live for a hundred years or more too.
The oldest land animal is a giant tortoise called Jonathan who's 183.

But adult mayflies only live for about five minutes.

GIANT SPIDER AT... NOW!

Some spiders have to live their whole life in a year.
Others, like the goliath birdeating spider, can live for 20 years.

Sponges live for thousands of years.
Clams can live for hundreds.
And one type of lobster never ages.
But one species can live FOREVER!
The immortal jellyfish.

It's my 1000th birthday

Sponge

Sponge Cake

Hundreds of years buried in sand! Call that living?

clam

I'm immortal!

I'm not!

Turritopsis Dohrnii

Moulting every year for 30 years!! I'm over it.

This lobster doesn't age, but dies while moulting after about 30 years.

The reason we can't live forever is AGEING.

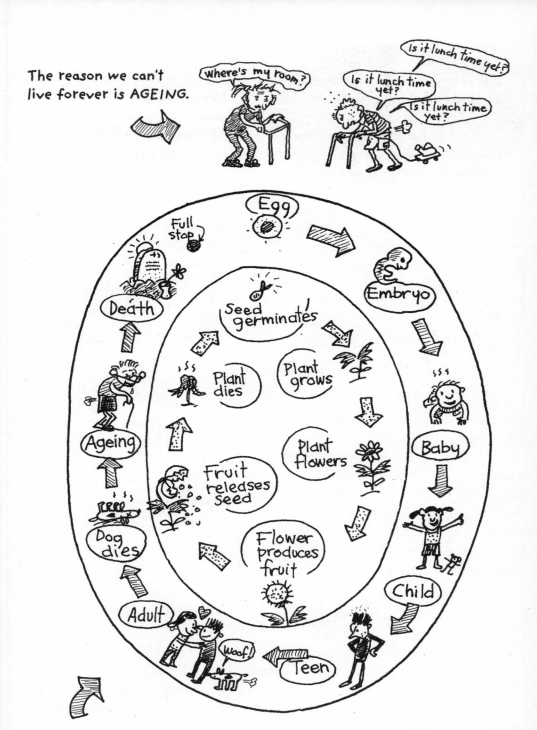

LIFE CYCLES

Ageing happens at different rates for different living things.

Life has only been on our planet for a REALLY short time compared to how long the Universe has been around.

It's just as hard to imagine the enormity of time as it is to imagine how many stars there are or how big space is or how small sub-atomic particles are.

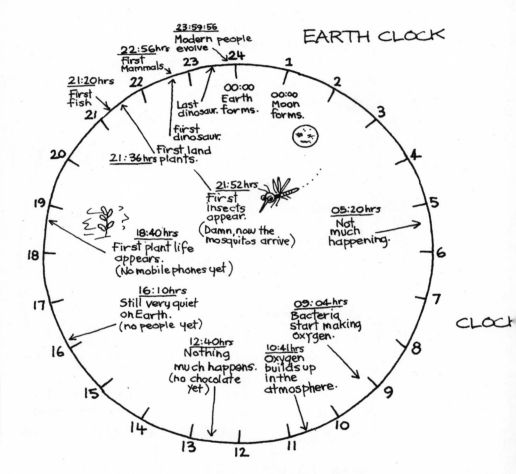

EARTH CLOCK

23:59:56 Modern people evolve

22:56hrs First Mammals

21:20hrs First fish

00:00 Earth forms.

00:00 Moon forms.

Last dinosaur forms.

First dinosaur.

First land plants. 21:36hrs

21:52hrs First insects appear. (Damn, now the mosquitos arrive)

05:20hrs Not much happening.

18:40hrs First plant life appears. (No mobile phones yet)

16:10hrs Still very quiet on Earth. (no people yet)

09:04hrs Bacteria start making oxygen.

12:40hrs Nothing much happens. (no chocolate yet)

10:41hrs Oxygen builds up in the atmosphere.

CLOC

Humans have only been around for a fraction of a second on the Earth clock. Who knows how long our species will last?

Even our wonderful star, the Sun,
will EVENTUALLY age and die.

Stars like the Sun usually burn
for about 9 or 10 billion years.

And ours is about 4.5 billion years old.

So in about 5 billion years,
when the Sun is very old,
it will become
a RED GIANT . . .

It will expand out towards Earth
and swallow it up,
along with Mercury, Venus and Mars.

The
Sun

Big hot
thing →

Earth →

But our TOUGH rocky little planet might still survive.

Even when the Sun is really REALLY old
and all that's left is a dim, cool WHITE DWARF,
Earth might still be around.

Eventually, though, whatever is left of Earth will float off into
space to take its chances against asteroids and black holes.

Life around us is always about beginnings and endings.
But the Sun is only a young star and the end is ages away.
Will the UNIVERSE ever end? We don't know.

We just know it started **14 BILLION YEARS AGO** with the . . .

Scientists know that from studying light
and the other radiation that comes from deep space.
It shows that since the Big Bang the Universe
has been cooling and expanding.

BEFORE THE BEGINNING

But what was there
BEFORE the Big Bang?

Maybe there was NOTHING.
NO matter and NO time.
What would that be like?

The science of the Universe is filled with very BIG IDEAS

In this chapter you have
to imagine
the UNIMAGINABLE!

Are you ready?

Scientists say that if you could press
the rewind button on the Universe
and watch time going in reverse,
you would see the Universe
getting smaller and smaller.

Eventually it would be unbelievably small,
much, much smaller than even the smallest sub-atomic particle.

Scientists call what was there before the Big Bang
THE SINGULARITY.

The singularity would have been very dense.
A tiny ball of heat and energy that contained all the mass
and all the space-time that now makes up our WHOLE UNIVERSE.

The singularity magnified
1,000,000,000,000,000,000,
000,000,000,000,000000,
000,000,000,000,000,000,
000,000,000,000,000,000,
000,000,000,000,000,000,
000,000,000,000,000,000,
000,000,000,000,000,000,
000,000,000,000,000,000,
000,000,000,000,000,000,
and a half times.

That MIGHT mean
that time didn't exist yet.

Or it might mean that time
DID exist.
It was just DIFFERENT.

Time might not have gone in just one direction back then.
It might have gone in all directions
and created many PARALLEL UNIVERSES.

So our Universe might be just one part of something even BIGGER.
And . . .
different versions of you might exist in other universes,
living different versions of your life.

But what if time . . .

HAD NO BEGINNING
AND HAS NO END?

NOW THAT'S
A BIG
IDEA!

Maybe time is a bit like a Mobius strip.

This Mobius strip is doing my head in!

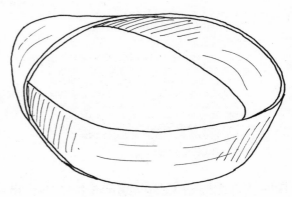

You can make a Mobius strip by twisting a strip of paper together at the ends so it looks like this picture.

Now imagine an ant walking along one surface. It could walk forever, but the strip would never end.

Stupid ants.

Time COULD be a bit like that.

FACT BOX

CLASSICAL PHYSICS, the science of Isaac Newton (remember him?), uses maths to tell us how things work in the world we can see and interact with. QUANTUM PHYSICS tells us about the things that are too small for us to experience. It's still about matter and energy, but it's the science of the super, super tiny — atoms and sub-atomic particles.

Time in our world is a big arrow moving at the same speed only in one direction.

But IS it? In the early 1900s Albert Einstein came up with the THEORY OF RELATIVITY. His theory says that time moves slower as the gravity increases on the thing experiencing time. And going faster slows time too.

Einstein WASN'T talking about how time slows down in the last fifteen minutes of class.

He called it TIME DILATION.
Scientists can prove it REALLY DOES HAPPEN.
It's like the tides, though.
You won't notice it happening in your everyday life.

Time is a jet plane.

When scientists sent an atomic clock into orbit, it really did come back running behind the one that stayed on Earth.

Welcome home, Sis.

Bub... Flub... Dub...

Time went slower when the clock was moving faster.
That means that you could travel forward in time faster than someone else.

Imagine a baby astronaut who has travelled close to the speed of light. If she had a twin who stayed at home, the baby astronaut would come home much younger than her twin.
Her twin on Earth would have aged at the 'normal' rate.

Einstein's Theory of Relativity
says that if you go FASTER than
light you can travel BACK in time too.

Hey, Bird that means Time travel is **REAL**!

Let's do it!

WOW! That means I could travel back to my own egg!

Let's TRAVEL *IN* TIME!

Sadly there IS a problem. And it's a biggie.

This is too easy for monkeys!

We are made of ATOMS.
And even though atoms are mostly nothing,
they are still definitely SOMETHING.
That something is called MATTER.
Light is ENERGY, not matter.
It is made of things called PHOTONS.

Matter has to obey the rules of physics.
But light doesn't.

Einstein's equation $E = MC^2$
means that if you have mass (which we do and light doesn't)
the faster you go the heavier you get.
And getting heavier means you need more and more energy
to keep going faster.
If you could get close to the speed of light,
your mass would be HUGE.

After that it would be INFINITE .

So it's not possible to go faster than light.
Light will always win the race.

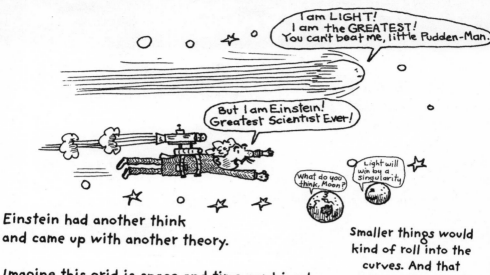

Einstein had another think
and came up with another theory.

Imagine this grid is space and time combined.

Smaller things would
kind of roll into the
curves. And that
would explain why the
Universe has gravity.

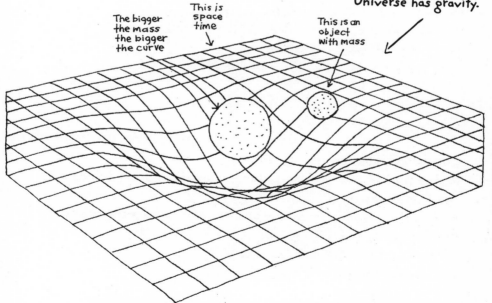

This also means there could be WORMHOLES in space-time.
Tunnels connecting places and times usually very far apart.

TIME TRAVEL IS . . .

. . . POSSIBLE if you want to age at a different speed to anyone else.

If time travel is possible, Bird, where are all the tourists from the future?

Good question, Horse.

But HIGHLY UNLIKELY if you want to go back to last Saturday.

Goal!

Or to last century to meet Albert Einstein.

Go, Albie!!

I got rhythm!

Or to the Jurassic to race a velociraptor.

Or back billions of years to check out the first life on Earth.

Or to the singularity to find out what was there before the Big Bang.

INFINITY AND BEYOND!

Even travelling forward in time by going super fast would be hard.
And probably fatal.

If you speed up, slow down or make a sudden turn,
your body has to deal with G-FORCES.
You can feel gs when you're on a rollercoaster.

Too many gs can break your bones,
burst your soft squishy organs,
or send all your blood to your brain (ewww).

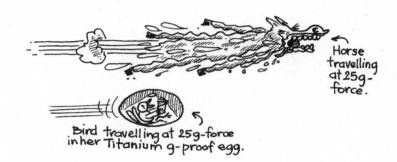

Horse
travelling
at 25g-
force.

Bird travelling at 25g-force
in her Titanium g-proof egg.

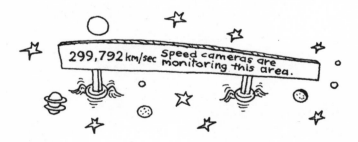

299,792 km/sec Speed cameras are
monitoring this area.

Also the faster we go in space, the more likely we are to hit
REALLY HARD something going REALLY FAST in the other direction.
Like tiny meteors going at about 300,000 kilometres per hour.
At that speed they're basically super-powerful space bullets.

The fastest humans have ever flown was on the Apollo 10 space mission. And those astronauts only went 39,897 km per HOUR. Nowhere near the 299,792 km per SECOND that light goes in a vacuum.

Even if you COULD travel through time, what would you do?

You couldn't time travel to the past to CHANGE anything, because then it wouldn't have happened. And you wouldn't have travelled in time to STOP it happening.

And what if you changed something ACCIDENTALLY? Like your time machine squashed your future self?

Or worse! What if you travelled to the past and squashed your ten-year-old grandpa?

He would never grow up and never have kids, and you would never have been born.

Sorry Grandpa Me, but this never really happened.

Badly drawn Professor's hat

Then why is my back so sore?

Tooth

The good news is then you wouldn't EXIST to travel in time and squash him. That's called a PARADOX.

Thank goodness you can't time travel, or you might have been trapped in a big fat TIME LOOP instead of reading this book!

7

I HOPE YOU WERE PAYING ATTENTION BECAUSE THERE WILL BE A TEST

Okay, I'll admit it . . .
I'm TOO KIND.

THERE IS

NO...

TEST

Instead, here are all the answers to
the questions of the universe . . .

and the meaning of life thrown
in for free!

The Universe is a very BIG thing,
yet at the beginning it was so small
you couldn't see it.

Then it BIG BANGED!

YOU are a small thing full of
really tiny things.
But compared to those tiny things
you are as big as the Universe.

The Universe is 14 billion years old.
Earth is 4.5 billion years old.
So for billions of years not much happened.
Then people arrived.
Not by alien invasion,
but by evolution.

After a while people invented
fire, agriculture, stuff, cars, planes,
medicine, electric lights, TV, rockets,
internet and CHOCOLATE.

But none of these things would
have been invented if we hadn't
first invented communication,
co-operation and FRIENDSHIP.

And we will never do better than that!

So,
REALLY,
    THIS
        IS . . . .